RONAYNE'S HAND-BOOK
OF
FREEMASONRY

BY

EDMOND RONAYNE

ISBN: 978-1-63923-466-0

Printed: AUGUST 2022

Cover Art By: Amit Paul

Published and Distributed By:
Lushena Books
607 Country Club Drive, Unit E
Bensenville, IL 60106
www.lushenabooksinc.com/books

ISBN: 978-1-63923-466-0

Fraternally yours
Edmund Romayne

RONAYNE'S HAND-BOOK

OF

FREEMASONRY

WITH APPENDIX

REVISED—ENLARGED—COMPLETE.

Containing a Thorough Exposition of all the Signs, Grips,
Passwords and Hieroglyphics used by Freemasons; also
the Proper Manner of Opening, Closing and Conducting the Lodge, together with the Correct
Method of Conferring the Three Degrees
of "Ancient Craft Masonry"; Entered   Apprentice,   Fellow
Craft and Master Mason

BY

EDMOND RONAYNE

Late Past Master of Keystone Lodge, No. 639, Chicago,
Ill. Author of "Master's Carpet," "Masonic Oaths" and
"Chapter Masonry."

THE GAME OF KNOWLEDGE
P.O. Box 496292
Chicago, IL 60649-6292
Reprinted 2001

RONAYNE'S HANDBOOK OF

FREEMASONRY

WITH APPENDIX

REVISED—ENLARGED—ILLUSTRATED

BY

EDMOND RONAYNE

Past Master of Keystone Lodge, No. 639
Author of "The Master's Carpet" and
"Chapter Masonry"

THE PLATE OF KNIGHTFIELD

P.O. Box 49267
Chicago, IL 60649
Reprinted 2001

NOMENCLATURE AND CLASSIFICATION OF THE GRADES IN FREEMASONRY

SYMBOLIC GRADES

Conferred only in regular Lodges of Master Masons, duly constituted by Grand Lodges

1° Entered Apprentice   2° Fellowcraft
3° Master Mason

INEFFABLE GRADES

4° Secret Master	9° Master Elect of Nine
5° Perfect Master	10° Master Elect of Fifteen
6° Intimate Secretary	11° Sublime Master Elected
7° Provost and Judge	12° Grand Master Architect
8° Intendant of the building	13° Master of the Ninth Arch

14° Grand Elect Mason

Conferred in a Lodge of Perfection, 14°, duly constituted under authority of the Supreme Council of the 33°.

ANCIENT HISTORICAL AND TRADITIONAL GRADES

15° Knight of the East or   16° Prince of Jerusalem
Sword

Conferred in a Council, Princes of Jerusalem, 16°.

APOCALYPTIC AND CHRISTIAN GRADES

17° Knight of the East and West
18° Knight of Rose Croix de H-R-D-M
Conferred in a Chapter of Rose Croix
de H-R-D-M, 18°

MODERN HISTORICAL, CHIVALRIC, AND PHILOSOPHICAL GRADES

19° Grand Pontiff	27° Commander of the Temple
20° Master ad Vitam	28° Knight of the Sun
21° Patriarch Noachite	29° Knight of St. Andrew
22° Prince of Libanus	30° Grand Elect Kadosh or Knight of the White and
23° Chief of the Tabernacle	Black Eagle
24° Prince of the Tabernacle	31° Grand Inspector
25° Knight of the Brazen Serpent	Inquistor Commander
26° Prince of Mercy	32° Sublime Prince of the Royal Secret

Conferred in a Consistory, Sublime Princes of the Royal Secret, 32°

OFFICIAL GRADES

33° Sovereign Grand Inspector General

Conferred only by the SUPREME COUNCIL, 33°, and upon those who may be elected to receive it by that high body which assembles yearly.

PREFACE TO REVISED EDITION

———

Notwithstanding the claim made by the old authors of Masonic literature, that the Ritual of Freemasonry does not change, there has, within a few years, been a radical change in the phraseology of the Ritual, and some changes in the formula of conducting the lodge ceremonies. To meet these changes this handbook has been revised to correspond with present formulas, and, it is believed, will be found correct in every essential particular.

In performing this service the editor has been ably assisted by a man who recently has been a member of the Order, and is thoroughly posted on its workings.

T. B. ARNOLD.

Glen Ellyn, Illinois, February 15th, 1917

AUTHOR'S PREFACE, 1904

The great Chicago fire occurred on the 8th and 9th of October, 1871. At that time I was secretary of Keystone Lodge, No. 639 A. F. & A. M., our meetings being held every Wednesday night at the corner of Wells and Ohio streets on the North Side. Our hall was destroyed but I saved all the paraphernalia of the Lodge, not even a scrap of paper being missing; on that account receiving a unanimous vote of thanks, which with a series of resolutions were "spread on the Minutes," and which doubtless to this day form a part of the lodge record of that trying time.

Immediately after the fire a few of us took temporary charge of the Masonic supplies coming in from Louisville, Kentucky, and other places, establishing our relief headquarters in the Masonic building near the corner of West Randolph and Halsted streets, and began at once to supply as best we could, the most pressing wants of our burned-out brother Master Masons and the widows and orphans of deceased Masons. In about a week or ten days the Grand Master, De Witt C. Cregier, organized a regular Board of Masonic Relief, of which I was an active member from the very first, and so continued until the labors of the Board were no longer necessary,—a period of eight months, ending June 24, 1872. (See Appendix, page 273.)

At the regular communication of Keystone Lodge in December, 1871, I was unanimously elected Senior Warden, and began at once to make preparation to hold a weekly Masonic school of instruction for the special benefit of the members of the lodge. With that object in view, I used to have stated rehearsals in the ritual and lectures with H. F. Holcomb and George R. McClellen of Lodge 141 and with D. H. Kilmore of 209, all Past Masters of their respective lodges and District Deputy Grand Masters of Chicago districts. But to make assurance doubly sure, I used to call at least once a week upon Brother Edward Cook, one of the "Grand Examiners" in the Illinois Grand Lodge, and conceded to be one of the best posted Masons in the United States for special examination and instruction in the entire work of conferring the three symbolic degrees.

My knowledge of the alleged "secret work" of Freemasonry then was acquired not from any *second-hand* source, or by guessing at the meaning of hieroglyphic characters in a so-called *Masonic key*, but direct from the fountain head, the official custodians of the "Standard Work."

And thus possessing an absolutely accurate knowledge of both the MONITORIAL and SECRET WORK it was my privilege once every week to meet with the officers of Keystone Lodge, and other Masons who could attend and conduct a "Masonic school of instruction," which we kept up regularly until June 24th, 1874. Precisely as I received the Masonic work from the Grand Examiners and District Grand Masters, and precisely as I taught it to the officers of Keystone Lodge and others so I have written it word for word in the Hand Book of Freemasonry and hence the Masons, not alone of Chicago, but throughout the country at large, are using it to-day and have used it as a private text-book for more than a quarter of a century. Very often I receive a letter addressed simply to E. Ronayne, Keystone Lodge 639, Chicago, and quite recently a letter came from Masonic Lodge, No. 86, Red Bird, I. T., addressed merely to E. Ronayne, 639, Chicago, Illinois.

At the annual meeting of Keystone Lodge, No. 639, in December, 1872, I was elected Worshipful Master by a practically unanimous vote and thus by virtue of my official position became an active, voting member of the Grand Lodge of Illinois, and at the close of my official term in January, 1874, the lodge presented me with a beautiful Past Master's regalia, consisting of a collar, apron and jewel, and seventy-five dollars in cash.

Mr. Edward Cook, above referred to, is now Past Grand Master of Masons of Illinois, having been a few years ago, twice elected to the high office of Grand Master. All these facts go to prove beyond any peradventure that the following pages contain an absolutely accurate reproduction of the Standard Ritual and Work of Ancient Craft Masonry.

For a full explanation of the Masonic ceremonies and symbols (the real secret of Masonry) the reader is referred to the author's other book, "The Master's Carpet."

E. RONAYNE.

104 *Milton avenue, Chicago, Illinois, March 23, 1904.*

CONTENTS

CONTENTS

CONTENTS.

HAND BOOK OF FREEMASONRY

A COMPLETE LODGE MANUAL

INTRODUCTION.

A Lodge of Freemasons is organized as follows. —A sufficient number of well known brethern,—no fewer, at least, than eight,—in good standing, or holding *demits* from some other regular Lodge, send a petition to the Grand Master of the State or Territory in which they reside, setting forth that they desire to organize a Lodge of Free and Accepted Masons at such-and-such a place, for the purpose of practicing the mysteries and inculcating the doctrines and principles of Freemasonry. This petition should also state the name of their first Worshipful Master, who *must* be either a *present* or *past* Warden, or Past Master; and it must be further accompanied with a plan of the Lodge-room and its location and surroundings. The usual fee prescribed by the by-laws of the Grand Lodge must also be transmitted,—in Illinois, it is $100. All necessary requirements having been thus complied with, the Grand Master, issues a dispensation, authorizing them to open a Lodge of Master Masons, and to *initiate, craft* and *raise,* according to ancient usage, until the next meeting of the Grand Lodge.

1

When first organized in this manner, it is termed a "Lodge U. D.," because working, *under dispensation*, and, enjoys no other Masonic privilege than merely that of conferring the three degrees of symbolic Masonry.   At the next meeting of the Grand Lodge, however, it must transmit its *dispensation* to that body, and also its Record Book, in order that its "work" may be properly examined and passed upon; and if everything is found to be regular, and the degrees conferred according to the standard ritual of Masonry, the Grand Lodge authorizes a "charter" to be issued, and the new lodge is cheerfully admitted into the family of constituent Lodges of the jurisdiction over which the Grand Lodge is the supreme governing body.

Immediately after the granting of the "charter," an election of officers is usually held; and as soon thereafter as possible, either the Grand Master or his Deputy, constitutes the new Lodge by installing its officers "according to ancient usage."

From this brief description, then, it will be seen that Masonic Lodges are of two kinds,—"Lodges U. D.," and "Chartered Lodges."   The former, as already stated, enjoy no privilege beyond that of conferring the degrees; while a chartered Lodge exercises all the functions, and enjoys all the privileges, granted by the Landmarks of the Order.   It is as well established a fact as anything can possibly be, that Freemasonry is a consummate swindle from beginning to end,—a deliberate fraud through and through; and hence it would make a curious chapter in Masonic history if, when a new lodge is formed, a brief account of its organization could be published. The public then could see whether Freemasons' Lodges are established for the general good, or whether they

are not, in the majority of cases, organized by design-
ing tricksters,—men whom Masonry makes cunning,
—for their own selfish purposes, and because they have
been either dissatisfied or disgusted with the way
things have been running in their own old Lodge.

As a specimen of the benevolence and philan-
thropy actuating the members of the Masonic institution in the formation of new Lodges, I shall here
transcribe the official report of the Finance Committee
of Keystone Lodge, No. 639, rendered at its first "annual communication" after its charter was granted and
the Lodge duly constituted. I shall give this report
verbatim et literatim; and while the Masonic reader
will readily recognize in it a very fair specimen of the
charity and brotherly love existing among the members
of the Craft, the uninitiated profane will be able to
answer that question which we hear almost daily propounded, "What becomes of all the Masonic money?"
I ought to add further, perhaps, that the Lodge received its charter on the 9th day of October, 1869,
when the Grand Lodge met at Springfield, Ill., and
when Harmon G. Reynolds was Grand Master; and
that the following "report" was presented on January
3d, 1870. Here is the document:—

*"To Worshipful Master, Wardens and Brethren, Key-
stone Lodge, No. 639:*

"Your Finance Committee respectfully submit the following report, as the transactions of this Lodge
for the last Masonic year:

	Dr.	Cr.
27 Charter Members as reported by M. Shields..................	$135.00	
33 Petitions for membership rec'd by the Lodge...............	165.00	

17 Entered Apprentices initiated, @
    $20.00 .... 340.00
13 Fellow Crafts passed, @ 20.00 260.00
12 Master Masons raised, @ 20.00 240.00
Dues from Stamme 4.25
Vouchers paid by Treasurer, and so
    ordered by the Lodge, per Ex-
    hibit A .... $ 567.13
Vouchers paid by Treasurer, and so
    ordered by Bro. M. Shields, and
    not ordered by the Lodge, and
    stated as expenses to Spring-
    field:
Voucher No. 45, Drft. d r a w n a t
                Springfield, in fa-
                vor of J. P. Ferns,
                G. Tyler 20.00
Voucher No. 33 for Grand Lodge
                dues and Charter 100.00
Voucher No. 35 on acc't of Grand
                Lodge expense... 40.00
Voucher No. 36 for obtaining Char-
                ter 75.00
Voucher No. 38 for obtaining Dis-
                pensation 90.00
Voucher No. 47 for expenses for
                Charter & other. 103.00

                     $1,144.25 $995.13
The amount of money in Treasury 6.75
Am't held by Sec'ty Leo Canman
    and not paid over to Treasurer 142.35

                    $1,144.25 $1,144.25

Total amount of money received by
    Sec'y of this Lodge to June
    1st, 1869 ....$1,144.25

The amount of money paid over to
    Treasurer by Sec'ty, and for
    which he holds receipts of
    treasurer $960.00

Am't still in Treasury............   6.75

Deficiency in money rec'd by Sec'y
    and what was paid over by
    him to Treasurer 177.50

                                  $1,144.25 $1,144.25

Expense of W. Bros. M. Shields to
    Springfield and back to obtain
    charter, &c. $428.00

The expense to Springfield and
    back for two trips should be... $35.00

Dispensation 9.00

Charter 25.00

6 days board, @ $4.00 per day.....   24.00

Over charges to Springfield 335.00

                                     $428.00 $428.00

                Wm. Sanderson, ⎫
                J. H. Dixon,   ⎬ COMMITTEE
                C. H. Didiriksen,⎭

With regard to this official document, it will be
sufficient to remark that it indelibly stamps every single transaction in the organization of Keystone Lodge,
No. 639, as a wilful and deliberate steal, from beginning to end. First, every candidate was defrauded in
the sum of $64.25, by being charged $65, in all, for
his three degrees, when the officers and members of

that Lodge knew, just as well as they did their own names, that those very same degrees,—word for word, and in better form,—could be purchased of any regular book-seller in the country for 75 cents at most.

Secondly, the money thus fraudulently obtained from "the poor, blind candidate," was in its turn stolen by Moses Shields, their Worshipful Master, and by others, thus very forcibly proving the truth of that old adage—"Ill got, ill gone."

Thirdly, the Grand Lodge of Illinois, for the sum of $75, gave them permission to open their Masonic confidence shop and to sell Masonic so-called secrets to any white man of mature age, who might be foolish enough to buy them, thus encouraging and perpetuating the fraud by issuing its charter or warrant, empowering them to work.

In this manner, Freemason Lodges are organized and the money filched from the poor, selfish, deluded dupes who join them, is disposed of. Every Masonic Lodge in the world is a fraud; the sale of its sham degrees is but obtaining money under false pretenses; and what is still worse, the Masons themselves know it. This being the case, then, and desiring to do what I can towards exposing the swindle and the outrageous humbug of these dark gangs of conspiracy, I would earnestly call the reader's attention to the following pages, as containing the literally correct *ritual* and *work* of Freemasonry.

CHAPTER I.

OPENING CEREMONIES.

As has been already intimated, the presiding officer of a Lodge of Masons, and in fact its supreme head, for the time being, is the Worshipful Master. Next to him in official rank is the Senior Warden; and next to him, the Junior Warden. These officers always occupy stations in the East, West, and South, respectively,—the Lodge-room being situated due East and West,—and in the religious symbolism of Freemasonry, they represent the sun at his rising, his meridian, and his setting. The other officers of the Lodge are the Treasurer, Secretary, Senior Deacon, Junior Deacon and Tyler, and take rank after the Wardens in the order in which they are here enumerated, and occupy positions as represented on page 20. A Senior and Junior Steward are also generally appointed, and sometimes a Chaplain and Organist, though in most Lodges, these latter are usually dispensed with. The Stewards sit at the right and left, and a little to the front, of the Junior Warden.

On entering a Masonic Lodge, the first object that will particularly attract one's attention is the *altar,* situated in the center of the room, midway between the East and West, and hence directly opposite the South, as seen on page 20. Near the *altar* it will be noticed that there are three burning tapers,—either candles or gas jets or electric lights,—which are also situated so as to point towards the East, West, and

7

South, as seen in the accompanying figure, and must be always lighted before the Lodge is opened. On the *altar* there is also a copy of the Holy Bible,—closed, as yet,—and on the Bible we find invariably the Square

and Compass.* The hour prescribed in the by-laws for opening the Lodge having arrived, and a sufficient number of the members being present,—eight at least, —they all clothe themselves in their proper regalia, which, for simple members, is *only a white linen apron,* and for the Worshipful Master and other officers, in addition to the apron is a *jewel* pertaining to each particular office, as explained hereafter. All things being thus in readiness, the Master *taps* the gavel, when both officers and members at once repair to their respective places and take their seats, as seen on page 20. Before the Worshipful Master himself takes his seat, however, he issues the following command:

Worshipful Master: 1 rap. "Brother Junior Deacon, you will see that the Tyler is at his post, and close the door."

Junior Deacon (looking into the ante-room to see if the Tyler is there, closes the door and replies) "The Tyler is at his post, Worshipful."

The Lodge is now ready to be opened in *due Form,* which must be always according to the order here laid down—the three following ceremonies being invariably performed :—

---

*For the position of God's Word in the Masonic Lodge see the "Master's Carpet," pp. 123-126.

PURGING THE LODGE.

Worshipful Master (giving one rap) : "Brother Senior Warden, are all present Masons?"

Senior Warden : 1 rap. "I will inquire by my proper officer and report." 1 rap. "Brother Junior Deacon, you will proceed to satisfy yourself that all present are Masons."

The Junior Deacon then taking his rod, proceeds around the Lodge-room, stopping in front of every brother whom he does not personally know, and raps on the floor with his rod; and that brother thus challenged, if not vouched for by some one present, must retire into the ante-room to await, if he sees fit, the action of an examining committee sent out by the W. M. The Junior Deacon, in this manner having made the entire circuit of the Lodge-room, returns in front of the Senior Warden's station, and reports to that officer: "I am so satisfied Bro. S. W.," and then resumes his former place in the Lodge. The Senior Warden then reports: "All present are Masons, Worshipful."*

Worshipful Master (speaking to S. W.) : "You will call the brethren to order as Entered Apprentice Masons, reserving yourself for the last."

Senior Warden (giving three raps) : "Brethren, you will come to order as Entered Apprentice Masons."

All the members rise to their feet and make the "due-guard" of an Entered Apprentice, as seen in the figure on page 10; after which, the Senior Warden makes the same sign, and reports :

Senior Warden : "In Order, Worshipful."

---

*For the origin and meaning of this ceremony, see "Master's Carpet," pp. 247-8.

The Worshipful Master then gives one rap, and the Lodge is seated.

The foregoing ceremony is by Masons technically called, "purging the Lodge," and must on no account be dispensed with or omitted.

TYLING THE LODGE.

Worshipful Master (gives one rap): "Brother Junior Deacon. The first great care of Masons when convened?"

Junior Deacon: "To see that the Lodge is tyled Worshipful."

Worshipful Master: "You will perform that duty, and inform the Tyler that I am about to open Keystone Lodge, No. 639 on the first degree of Masonry and direct him to take due notice, and tyle accordingly."

The Junior Deacon opens the door, without knocking, puts out his head and whispers to the Tyler, who is *standing* outside the door, that the lodge is about to be opened on the first degree. He then closes the door, and gives three distinct knocks, which are answered by the Tyler in like manner. The Junior Deacon then gives one knock, which is answered by one knock by the Tyler, when the Junior Deacon faces towards the East and reports as follows:

Junior Deacon: "The Lodge is tyled, Worshipful."

Worshipful Master: "How tyled?"

Junior Deacon: "By a Master Mason, armed with the proper implement of his office."

Worshipful Master: "The Tyler's station?"

Junior Deacon: "Outside the inner door, with a drawn sword in his hand." *

Worshipful Master: "His duty?"

Junior Deacon: "To guard against the approach of cowans and eaves-droppers, and see that none pass or repass, but such as are duly qualified, and have permission."

The Junior Deacon takes his seat.

LECTURING THE LODGE.

Worshipful Master (gives 1 rap): "Bro Senior Warden whence came you?"

Senior Warden: "From a Lodge of the Saints John of Jerusalem.*

Worshipful Master: "What came you here to do?"

Senior Warden: "To learn to subdue my passions and improve myself in Masonry."

Worshipful Master: "You are a Mason then, I presume."

Senior Warden: "I am, so taken and accepted among brothers and fellows."

Worshipful Master: "What makes you a Mason?"

---

* Why is the Tyler placed outside the Ante-room door? See "Master's Carpet," pp. 249.

* How could he come from a Lodge of the Saints John, when the Saints John never were Masons? See "Master's Carpet."

Senior Warden: "My obligation."

Worshipful Master: "How do you know your-selves to be a Mason?"

Senior Warden: "By having been often tried, never denied and being ready to be tried again."

Worshipful Master: "How shall I know you to be a Mason?"

Senior Warden: "By certain signs, a token, a word and the points of my entrance."

Worshipful Master: "What are signs?"

Senior Warden: "Right angles, horizonals and perpendiculars."

Worshipful Master: "What is a token?"

Senior Warden: "A certain friendly and broth-erly grip, whereby one Mason may know another in the dark as well as the light."

Worshipful Master: "Where were you made a Mason?"

Senior Warden: "In a regularly constituted Lodge of Masons."

Worshipful Master: "What number constitutes a Lodge of Masons."

Senior Warden: "Seven or more."

Worshipful Master: "When of seven, of whom do they consist?"

Senior Warden: "The Worshipful Master, Senior and Junior Wardens, Treasurer and Secretary, Senior and Junior Deacons."

Worshipful Master: "The Junior Deacon's place?"

Senior Warden: "At the right hand of the Senior Warden in the West."

The Worshipful Master gives two raps, which call all the officers to their feet.

Worshipful Master: "Your duty, brother Junior Deacon?"

Junior Deacon: "To carry *messages* from the Senior Warden in the West, to the Junior Warden in the South, and elsewhere around the Lodge, as directed; take charge of the door and with the assistance of the Stewards prepare and present candidates."

Worshipful Master: "Brother Junior Deacon, the Senior Deacon's place?"

Junior Deacon: "At the right hand, of the Worshipful Master in the East."

Worshipful Master: "Your duty, brother Senior Deacon?"

Senior Deacon: "To carry *orders* from the Worshipful Master in the East, to the Senior Warden in the West, and elsewhere around the Lodge, as required; to introduce and accommodate visiting brethren, receive and conduct candidates."

Worshipful Master: "Brother Senior Deacon, the Secretary's place?"

Senior Deacon: "On your left, Worshipful."

Worshipful Master: "Your duty, brother Secretary?"

Secretary: "To observe the will and pleasure of the Worshipful Master; record all the proceedings of the Lodge, proper to be written; transmit a copy of the same to the Grand Lodge, when required; receive all moneys paid into the Lodge, pay them over to the Treasurer, taking his receipt therefor."

Worshipful Master: "Brother Secretary, the Treasurer's place?"

Secretary: "On your right, Worshipful."

Worshipful Master: "Your duty, brother Treasurer?"

Treasurer: "To receive all moneys paid into the Lodge from the hands of the Secretary, keep a just and regular account of the same, pay them out by the order of the Worshipful Master and consent of the Lodge."

Worshipful Master: "Brother Treasurer, the Junior Warden's station?"

Treasurer: "In the South, Worshipful."

Worshipful Master: "Why in the South, brother Junior- Warden?"

Junior Warden: "As the sun in the South, at meridian height, the beauty and glory of the day, so is the Junior Warden in the South, the better to observe the time, to call the Craft from labor to refreshment; superintend them during the hour thereof; see that none convert the means of refreshment into intemperance or excess; call them to labor again, at the order of the Worshipful Master, that he may have pleasure, and the Craft profit thereby."

Worshipful Master: "Brother Junior Warden, the Senior Warden's station?"

Junior Warden: "In the West, Worshipful."

Worshipful Master: "Why in the West, brother Senior Warden?"

Senior Warden: "As the sun is in the West at the close of the day, so is the Senior Warden in the West to assist the Worshipful Master in opening and closing his Lodge; pay the Craft their wages, if any be due, so that none may go away dissatisfied, *harmony* being the *strength* and support of all institutions, especially ours."

Worshipful Master: "Brother Senior Warden the Worshipful Master's station?"

Senior Warden: "In the East, Worshipful."

Worshipful Master: "Why in the East?"

Senior Warden: "As the sun rises in the East to open and govern the day, so rises the Worshipful Master in the East" (here the Worshipful Master rises to his feet) "to open and govern his Lodge, set the Craft to work, and give them proper instructions."

Worshipful Master: "Brother Senior Warden, it is my order that Keystone Lodge, No. 639, be now opened on the first degree of Masonry; this you will communicate to the Junior Warden in the South, and he to the brethren, that all having due notice thereof, may govern themselves accordingly."

Senior Warden: "Brother Junior Warden, it is the order of the Worshipful Master that Keystone Lodge, No. 639, be now opened on the first degree of Masonry, this you will communicate to the brethren, that all having due notice thereof, may govern themselves accordingly."

Junior Warden (giving three raps, which call up the entire Lodge): "Brethren, it is the order of the Worshipful Master, communicated to me by the way of the West, that Keystone Lodge, No. 639, be now opened on the first degree of Masonry; take due notice thereof, and govern yourselves accordingly."

Worshipful Master: "Together, brethren."

Here the Master and all the members present, in concert make the due-guard and sign of an Entered Apprentice, the Master always leading off.

The due-guard is made by holding out the left hand a few inches from the body, and on a line with the lower button of the vest, with the palm open and turned upward. Now place the open palm of the right hand horizontally across the left, and about two or

three inches above it. (See fig.) This is in allusion
to the manner in which an Entered Apprentice's hands

Due-guard.

are placed while taking the obligation, "the left hand
supporting the Holy Bible, Square and Compass, and
the right resting thereon." (See Entered Apprentice's
obligation, page 69.)

Now drop the left hand carelessly, and draw the
right edgewise across the throat (palm open), and drop
it perpendicularly to your side. (See fig.) This is

called the "penal sign," or "sign of an Entered Apprentice," and alludes to the penalty of the obligation
—"having my throat cut across, my tongue torn out

by the roots," etc. (See Entered Apprentice's Obligation.)

The Worshipful Master immediately after making the sign, gives one rap with his gavel, the Senior Warden one, and the Junior Warden one; after which he proceeds:

Worshipful Master: "Brethren, before declaring the Lodge open, let us reverently invoke the blessing of Deity," and removing his hat, he repeats the following so-called prayer, as seen in the annexed figure. Let us pray.

WORSHIPFUL MASTER OPENING THE LODGF.

"Supreme Ruler of the universe, we would rev-

erently invoke thy blessing at this time. Wilt Thou
be pleased to grant that this meeting, thus begun in
order, may be conducted in peace, and closed in harmony. Amen. Response by the brethren: 'So mote
it be.' " Ordinarily used.

"Most holy and glorious Lord God, the great
Architect of the Universe, the giver of all good gifts
and graces: Thou hast promised that 'where two or
three are gathered together in Thy name, Thou wilt
be in their midst and bless them.' In Thy name we
have assembled, and in Thy name we desire to proceed in all our doings. Grant that the sublime principles of Freemasonry may so subdue every discordant passion within us, so harmonize and enrich our
hearts with Thine own love and goodness, that the
Lodge at this time may humbly reflect that order and
beauty which reign forever before Thy throne. Amen.
Response by the brethren: 'So mote it be.' "*

Worshipful Master: "Accordingly I declare Key-
stone Lodge, No. 639, opened on the first degree of
Masonry. Brother Junior Deacon, inform the Tyler.
Brother Senior Deacon, arrange the lights."

The Senior Deacon proceeds to the altar, situated
in the center of the room, opposite the Junior Warden's station, as already explained, opens the Bible,—
usually at Psalm 133,—and places upon it the Square
and Compass (the latter open), with both points of
the Compass *below* the Square, in the manner shown

* Cook's Standard Monitor, p. 6.

by the annexed cut, and returns to his place. The
Junior Deacon, at the same time, gives three knocks

at the door, which are answered by three from the
Tyler outside. The Junior Deacon then gives one,
which is answered by one from the Tyler. The door
is then opened, and the Junior Deacon whispers to the
Tyler that the Lodge is opened on the first degree;
after which he closes the door and reports to the Master: "The Tyler is informed, Worshipful;" when the
Master gives one rap, and the Lodge is seated.

On the next page will be found a correct representation of the positions occupied by the different officers of a Lodge, whether it be opened on the
first, second or third degree; and nothing needs to be
added further on that head, except to describe the
jewels of office which each officer must wear, and to
which brief allusion has already been made.

Past Master wears a compass, opened on a quarter circle, *sun* in the center.

Worshipful Master wears a square; Senior Warden, a level.

Junior Warden, a plumb; Treasurer, cross-keys.

Secretary, cross-pens; Senior Deacon, Square and
Compass, sun in the center.

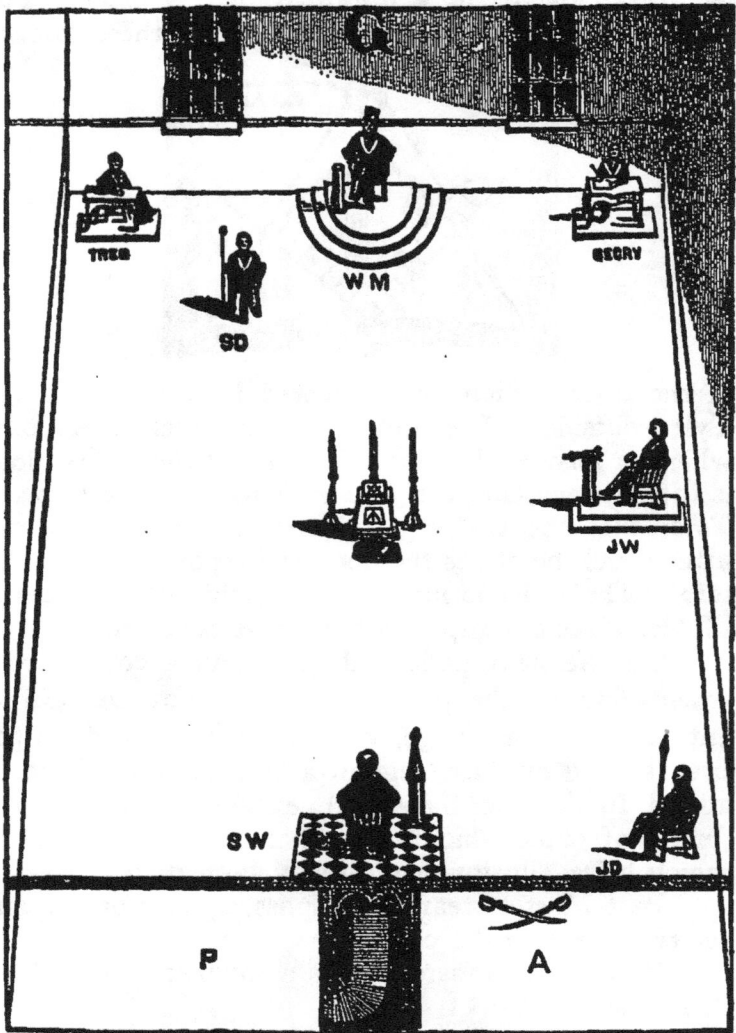

Junior Deacon, Square and Compass, quarter moon in center; Stewards, a cornucopia.

Chaplain, an open Bible; Tyler, a sword, saber shape.

If a collar is worn, these jewels must be suspended from the point of the collar; but if not, they are pinned to the right lapel of the coat.

The reader will also notice that a small pedestal stands to the right of the three principal officers, and that the Warden's columns rest upon those in the South and West. When the Lodge is open, the Senior Warden's column is standing up, as in the figure; but when the Lodge is called off, or during recess the Junior Warden's column is standing.

LODGE OF FELLOW CRAFTS.

OPENING CEREMONIES.

There is no material difference between an Entered Apprentice and a Fellow Craft Lodge. The officers in both cases are the same; the internal arrangements are the same; and a stranger, entering the Lodge-room while either degree is open, could not tell the difference, without carefully observing the position of the Square and Compass on the *altar*. In the first degree, as we have already seen, both points of the Compass are below the Square; while in the degree of Fellow Craft, one point is above, and another below, as seen on page 28. A Lodge of Fellow Crafts, however, cannot be opened without first opening a Lodge of Apprentices; and, as the design of these pages is to give the exact manner in which Masonry is worked, whether in opening or closing its Lodges, or in conferring its degrees; and as I have already given the correct method of opening a Lodge on the first degree; so I shall now proceed to open on the second.

PURGING THE LODGE.

Worshipful Master (one rap): "Brother Senior Warden, will you be off, or from?"

Senior Warden (rising): "From."

Worshipful Master: "From what, to what?"

Senior Warden: "From the degree of Entered Apprentice, to that of Fellow Craft."

Worshipful Master: "Are all present Fellow Crafts?"

Senior Warden: "I will inquire by my proper officer and report."

Senior Warden (one rap): "Brother Junior Deacon you will proceed to satisfy yourselves that all present are Fellow Crafts."

The Junior Deacon then taking his rod, proceeds around the Lodge-room, stopping in front of every brother whom he does not personally know, and raps on the floor with his rod; and that brother thus challenged, if not vouched for by some one present, must retire into the ante-room to await, if he sees fit, the action of an examining committee sent out by the W. M. The Junior Deacon, in this manner having made the entire circuit of the Lodge-room, returns in front of the Senior Warden's station, and reports to that officer: "I am so satisfied Bro. S. W.," and then resumes his former place in the Lodge.

Junior Deacon: "I am so satisfied Bro. Senior Warden."

Senior Warden (one rap) : "All present are Fellow Crafts, Worshipful."

Should there be one or more Entered Apprentices present. the Senior Warden will report: "All present are not Fellow Crafts, Worshipful." Upon which, the Master will request "all those below the degree of a Fellow Craft to please retire." Entered Apprentices then step to the altar, give the due-guard and sign, and retire to the ante-room.

Worshipful Master: "As a further evidence, you will cause the Senior and Junior Deacons to approach the West, receive from them the *pass,* direct them to proceed on the right and left, collect the *pass* from the brethren and convey it to the East."

Senior Warden (one rap) : "Brothers Senior and Junior Deacons, report to the West and give me the *pass* of a Fellow Craft."

The Senior and Junior Deacons both step to the altar, and from there approach the Senior Warden's station, to whom they communicate in a whisper the pass of a Fellow Craft—which is *Shibboleth.* They then cross to opposite sides of the hall (the Senior Deacon being on the right of the Senior Warden, and the Junior Deacon on his left), and in this manner they proceed to collect the pass from every member in the room, except the Master and Junior Warden. It ought to be observed that, in collecting this password, the Deacons are not to stoop down, so that a brother may whisper it while sitting; but they must stand erect, and every member must rise to his feet, whisper the pass-word, and again take his seat. Having thus collected the *pass,* they meet in front of the Master's chair, where they again cross to their respective sides of the Lodge-room; whereupon they face each other, and the Junior Deacon, making the due-guard of a Fellow Craft, gives the pass-word, *Shib-boleth,* to the Senior, and the Senior in the same manner to the Worshipful Master, who answers: "The pass is right;" and the Deacons return to their respective places.

I have been somewhat particular in describing this ceremony because, though simple in itself, I have met but very few Deacons who were able to perform it with neatness and precision; and further, because it is a ceremony which must on no occasion be omitted, either in the Grand Lodge or Blue Lodge.

Senior Warden to Junior Deacon and Senior Deacon, you will now proceed on the right and left, collect the pass from the brethren, and convey it to the East."

Worshipful Master (one rap): "The pass is right."

Worshipful Master: "Brother Senior Warden, are you a Fellow Craft?"

Senior Warden: "I am, try me."

Worshipful Master: "How will you be tried?"

Senior Warden: "By the Square."

Worshipful Master: "Why by the Square?"

Senior Warden: "Because it is an emblem of morality, and one of the working tools of a Fellow Craft."

Worshipful Master: "What is a Square?"

Senior Warden: "An angle of ninety degrees, or the fourth part of a circle."

Worshipful Master: "What makes you a Fellow Craft?"

Senior Warden: "My obligation."

Worshipful Master: "Where were you made a Fellow Craft?"

Senior Warden: "In a regularly constituted Lodge of Fellow Crafts."

Worshipful Master: "What number constitutes a Lodge of Fellow Crafts?"

Senior Warden: "Five or more."

Worshipful Master: "When of five only, whom do they consist?"

Senior Warden: "The Worshipful Master, Senior and Junior Wardens, Senior and Junior Deacons."

Worshipful Master: "The Junior Deacon's place?"

Senior Warden: "At the right hand of the Senior Warden in the West."

Worshipful Master (giving two raps, which call up the Senior and Junior Wardens, and the Senior and Junior Deacons): "Brother Junior Deacon, the Senior Deacon's place?"

Junior Deacon: "At the right hand, of the Worshipful Master in the East."

Worshipful Master: "Brother Senior Deacon, the Junior Warden's station?"

Senior Deacon: "In the South, Worshipful."

Worshipful Master: "Brother Junior Warden, the Senior Warden's station?"

Junior Warden: "In the West, Worshipful."

Worshipful Master: "Brother Senior Warden, the Worshipful Master's station?"

Senior Warden: "In the East, Worshipful."

Worshipful Masters "Why in the East?"

Senior Warden: "As the sun rises in the East to open and govern the day, so rises the Worshipful Master in the East" (Master rises to his feet) "to open and govern his Lodge, set the Craft to work and give them proper instruction."

Worshipful Master: "Brother Senior Warden, it is my order that Keystone Lodge, No. 639, be now opened on the *second* degree of Masonry. This you will communicate to the Junior Warden in the South, and he to the brethren, that all having due notice thereof, may govern themselves accordingly."

Senior Warden: "Brother Junior Warden, it is the order of the Worshipful Master that Keystone Lodge, No. 639, be now opened on the second degree of Masonry. This you will communicate to the brethren, that all having due notice thereof may govern themselves accordingly."

Junior Warden (three raps): "Brethren, it is the order of the Worshipful Master, communicated to me by the way of the West, that Keystone Lodge, No. 639, be now opened on the second degree of Masonry. Take due notice thereof, and govern yourselves accordingly."

Worshipful Master: "Together, brethren."

The Master leading off, and all the members present looking towards the East, then make the due-guard and sign of a Fellow Craft, as represented.

The due-guard of a Fellow Craft is made by holding out the right hand a few inches from the lower

Due-guard
Fellow Craft.

button of the vest, the fingers extended and the palms turned downward; raise the left arm so as to form a right angle at the elbow, with the fingers extended and the palm turned outward. This is in allusion to the position in which the hands are placed while taking the obligation, "My right hand resting on the Holy Bible, Square and Compass, my left forming a right angle," etc.

Now drop the left hand carelessly to the side, and draw the right hand with the fingers a little bent and turned inward, swiftly across the breast from left

Sign
Fellow Craft.

to right, and drop the hand perpendicularly to the side. This is called the sign of a Fellow Craft, and is in allusion to the penalty of the obligation, "Having my left breast torn open," etc. (See obligation of Fellow Craft, page 122.)

The Master gives two raps with his gavel, the Senior Warden two, and the Junior Warden two; after which the Master, removing his hat, exclaims:

Worshipful Master: "Accordingly, I declare

Keystone Lodge, No. 639, opened on the second degree of Masonry. Brother Junior Deacon, inform the Tyler. Brother Senior Deacon, arrange the lights.

The Senior Deacon now opens the Bible at the seventh Chapter of Amos, and places the Square and Compass upon it, with one point of the Compass above the Square, as in the figure.

Junior Deacon: "The Tyler is informed Worshipful."

Worshipful Master (gives one rap).

MASTER MASON'S LODGE.

OPENING CEREMONIES.

In the technical language of Masonry, a Lodge of Entered Apprentices represents the "ground floor" of King Solomon's Temple, a Lodge of Fellow Crafts, the "middle chamber," and a Lodge of Master Masons, the *"Sanctum Sanctorum,"* or Holy of Holies. In referring to the Jerusalem Temple, however, it must be borne in mind that every part of the Masonic system is symbolic, and consequently, that all allusions made in the ritual to Solomon's Temple, are only to be understood as symbolizing the erection of a spiritual temple in the heart, pure and spotless, which Freemasonry professes to build for every one of its members, Jew or Gentile, without the remotest reference to the name or atonement of Christ. In this way, and only in this, can the philosophy of Freemasonry and its true symbolism be rightly understood; and then it will be discovered that it is such a stupendous mass of infidelity and imposture, that modern civilization never witnessed its equal.

In opening a Master Mason's Lodge, the same rule must be observed as in the preceding case, and hence I shall now proceed to give the opening ceremonies of this sublime (?) degree in full:

Worshipful Master (one rap): "Brother Senior Warden, will you be off, or from?"

Senior Warden (rising): "From."

Worshipful Master: "From what, to what?"

Senior Warden: "From the degree of Fellow Craft to that of Master Mason."

Worshipful Master: "Are all present Master Masons?"

Senior Warden: "I will inquire by my proper officer and report."

Senior Warden (facing Junior Deacon) (one rap): "Brother Junior Deacon, you will proceed to satisfy yourselves that all present are Master Masons."

The Junior Deacon then taking his rod, proceeds around the Lodge-room, stopping in front of every brother whom he does not personally know, and raps on the floor with his rod; and that brother thus challegened, if not vouched for by some one present, must retire into the ante-room to await, if he sees fit, the action of an examining committee sent out by the W. M. The Junior Deacon, in this manner having made the entire circuit of the Lodge-room, returns in front of the Senior Warden's station, and reports to that officer: "I am so satisfied Bro. S. W.," and then resumes his former place in the Lodge. The Senior Warden then reports.

Senior Warden (one rap) : "All present are Master Masons, Worshipful."

Should there be any Fellow Crafts present, the Senior Warden replies: "All present are not Master Masons, Worshipful;" when the Master calls upon "all those below the degree of a Master to please retire." The Fellow Crafts will then step to the altar, make the due-guard and sign of that degree, and retire, as in the previous degree.

Worshipful Master: "As a further evidence, you will cause the Senior and Junior Deacons to approach the West, receive from them the *pass,* direct them to proceed on the right and left, collect the *pass* from the brethren and convey it to the East."

Senior Warden: "Bro. Senior and Junior Deacons, report to the West and give me the pass of a Master Mason. You will now proceed on the right and left collect the pass from the brethren and convey it to the East."

Worshipful Master (1 rap) : "The pass is right."

The Deacons approach the Senior Warden's station, as in the second degree, whisper into his ear the pass of a Master Mason, which is *Tubal-Cain;* they then go through the same performance exactly as they did in collecting the pass of a Fellow Craft, only using the due-guard of a Master Mason, and the Master makes the same response as before.

Worshipful Master: "Brother Senior Warden, are you a Master Mason?"

Senior Warden: "I am."

Worshipful Master: "What makes you a Master Mason?"

Senior Warden: "My obligation."

WORSHIPFUL MASTER.

JUNIOR WARDEN.

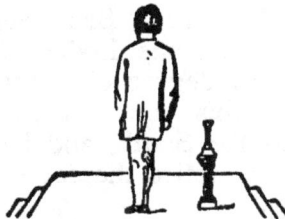

ALTAR.

SENIOR WARDEN.

To understand why the Master and Wardens are thus stationed, see "Master's Carpet" pp. 304—303.

Worshipful Master: "Where were you made a Master Mason?"

Senior Warden: "In a regularly constituted Lodge of Master Masons."

Worshipful Master: "What number constitutes a Lodge of Master Masons?"

Senior Warden: "Three or more."

Worshipful Master: "When of three, of whom do they consist?"

Senior Warden: "The Worshipful Master, Senior and Junior Wardens."

Worshipful Master: "The Junior Warden's station?"

Senior Warden: "In the South, Worshipful."

Worshipful Master (two raps): "Brother Junior Warden, the Senior Warden's station?"

Junior Warden: "In the West, Worshipful."

Worshipful Master: "Brother Senior Warden, the Worshipful Master's station?"

Senior Warden: "In the East, Worshipful."

Worshipful Master: "Why in the East?"

Senior Warden: "As the sun rises in the East to open and govern the day, so rises this Worshipful Master in the East to open and govern his Lodge, set the Craft to work, and give them proper instruction."

Worshipful Master: "Bro. Senior Warden, it is my order that Keystone Lodge, No. 639, be now opened on the third degree of Masonry for the dispatch of business, this you will communicate to the Junior Warden in the South, and he to the brethren, that all having due notice thereof may govern themselves accordingly."

Senior Warden (giving a slight rap): "Bro. Junior Warden, it is the order of the Worshipful Master that Keystone Lodge, No. 639, be now opened on the third degree of Masonry for the dispatch of business. This you will communicate to the brethren, that all having due notice thereof may govern themselves accordingly."

Junior Warden (giving three raps which call the brethren to their feet): "Brethren, it is the order of the Worshipful Master, communicated to me by the way of the West, that Keystone Lodge, No. 639, be now opened on the third degree of Masonry for the dispatch of business. Take due notice thereof, and govern yourselves accordingly."

Worshipful Master: "Together, brethren. (Alluding to the signs.)

Here the Worshipful Master and all the brethren in concert make the *due-guard* and *sign* of a Master Mason, as presented in the following figures.

The due-guard of a Master Mason is made by holding out both hands in front of the body, and on a line with the lower button of the vest, with fingers extended and palms downward. This is in allusion to the manner of holding the hands, while taking the

Due-guard
Master Mason.

Master Mason's obligation, "both hands resting on the Holy Bible, Square and Compass," etc See page 170.

Now drop the left hand carelessly, and draw the right across the body, fingers still extended and palm downward. (See fig.) This is the penal sign, and is in allusion to the penalty of the obligation of a Master

Penal Sign
Master Ma-
son.

Mason, "having my body severed in twain, my bowels taken from thence," etc. See Master Mason's obligation, page 170.

These signs being given as described, the Worshipful Master gives three raps, the Senior Warden three, and the Junior Warden three; after which the Master removes his hat and continues:

Worshipful Master: "Accordingly, I declare Keystone Lodge, No. 639, opened on the third degree of Masonry for the dispatch of business. Bro. Junior Deacon, inform the Tyler. Bro. Senior Deacon, arrange the lights."

The Worshipful Master then gives one rap, and all are again seated. The Lodge is now ready to proceed with its usual routine business, and at this stage of the proceedings, is correctly represented on the next page.

Junior Deacon: "The Tyler is informed, Worshipful."

Worshipful Master: 1 rap.

Keystone Lodge, No. 639, A.F.&A.M., in session, Jan. 14 '74

A-The Ante-room. P-The Preparation. *-The Tyler's Station

CHAPTER II.

VISITATION OF LODGES—GENERAL BUSINESS.

In relation to the foregoing ceremonies of opening the different Lodges of symbolic Masonry, among other things, it may be necessary to remark that in the Master's hand the gavel is the symbol of authority. As the reader has doubtless observed already, *one rap* calls the Lodge to order; *one rap* calls up any particular officer named; *two raps* call up all the officers named; and *three raps* call up the entire Lodge. This use of the gavel, therefor, by one, two, three, is invariably represented on the Lodge Chart,

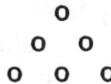

```
        o
     o     o
  o     o     o
```

or Master's Carpet, in the manner indicated in the margin, and though one of the first and simplest figures in Masonry, is a puzzle to nine-tenths of the members, so little do they really understand about an institution which costs them so much of valuable time and money, and which they have so solemnly sworn (as they suppose) to maintain and support.

Another marked feature of these opening ceremonies, is the utter absurdity, the silly, senseless twaddle, and the stupid, miserable nonsense connected with the whole business. And this is precisely what keeps Masonry alive, and causes it to flourish as it does; because the great majority of people can scarcely believe that judges, lawyers, ministers, bishops and shrewd, sensible business men will act so perfectly inconsistent and idiotic as to countenance for a single instant the endless repetition, and the ignorant, false and incoherent verbiage of the Masonic ritual. Just imagine one of the judges of our Supreme Court

replying to the question of a saloon keeper, if Worshipful Master, that he came "from a Lodge of the
Saints John at Jerusalem;" or a bishop declaring that
he became a Mason in order "to learn how to subdue his passions!"

ADMISSION OF VISITING BRETHREN.

The meetings of a Masonic Lodge are called
"communications." These are of two kinds, "regular," and "special." The "regular communications"
are those prescribed by the by-laws of the Lodge,
and at which its ordinary routine business is always
transacted; while a "special communication" is that
which is called by the Worshipful Master for some
special work, such as conferring degrees, conducting
a Masonic trial, etc. At "regular communications,"
visiting brethren, or strangers visiting the Lodge
usually wait till the Lodge is opened on the third
degree; but if it be a "special communication for
work," they always go in when the Lodge is open on
the degree to be conferred. To visit a Lodge, the following order must invariably be observed:

The visiting brother, unless otherwise vouched
for, approaches the ante-room door, and hands the
Tyler a card or slip of paper on which is written
his name, the name and number of his Lodge, and
the town or village where located. As for instance,
should I desire to visit a strange Lodge, I would
hand the Tyler a card inscribed as follows:

"EDMOND RONAYNE, Keystone Lodge, No. 639,
A. F. & A. M., Chicago."

The Tyler gives this card to the Junior Deacon,
and the latter, having obtained permission to approach
the East, hands it to the Worshipful Master, who

appoints a committee of two, usually a Past Master and some newly made Master Mason, to repair into the preparation or committee room, where the brother is strictly and searchingly examined on the ritual of Masonry. The examination always takes place as follows: The committee procure a Bible, Square and Compass, and they, with the visiting brother, placing their right hands upon them, repeat the following oath, called by Masons the

TEST OATH:

"I .... of my own free will and accord in the presence of Almighty God and these witnesses, do hereby and hereon most solemnly swear that I have been regularly initiated as an Entered Apprentice, passed to the degree of Fellow Craft, and raised to the sublime degree of Master Mason, in a regularly constituted Lodge of Masons, and that I am not now under the sentence of suspension or expulsion, and know of no just reason why I should not hold Masonic fellowship with by brethren, so help me God."

Having taken this "test oath," the committee and visitor resume their seats, and the examination is proceeded with, and is carried on as the senior member of the committee sees fit to conduct it; but the usual mode is, for the visiting brother to be examined in the lecture of the First Section of each degree, as given in Chapters IV., VI., IX. Being satisfied that the brother is all right, they return into the Lodge-room, approach the *altar,* make the due-guard and sign of a Master Mason, and report:

Committee: "Worshipful Master, your committee have examined brother E. Ronayne, of Keystone

Lodge, No. 639, Chicago, find him a Master Mason, in good standing, and recommend his admission."

They then take their seats.

Worshipful Master: "Brother Senior Deacon, you will retire and introduce brother E. Ronayne."

The Senior Deacon takes his rod, steps to the altar, salutes the Master with the due-guard and sign as usual, retires into the ante-room, and brother E. Ronayne having put on a white apron, and having signed his name in the register,—a book always used in the ante-room for that purpose,—he is conducted into the Lodge and before the Altar by the Senior Deacon, who announces as follows:

Senior Deacon! "Worshipful Master, I have the pleasure of introducing to you, brother E. Ronayne, of Keystone Lodge, No. 639, Chicago."

The Worshipful Master rises to his feet, gives three raps to call up the entire Lodge, and says:

Worshipful Master: "Brother E. Ronayne, I have the pleasure of introducing to you the officers and members of — Lodge, No. —, together with our visiting brethren; hope you will make yourself at home, while with us, and will visit us again whenever convenient," or words to that effect.

The Lodge is again seated, and the visitor is then conducted by the Senior Deacon to his seat. Should the visitor be a Past Master, or Grand officer, he is invited to take a seat in the East, either to the right or left of the Worshipful Master.

ORDINARY BUSINESS.

Under this head it may perhaps be proper to observe that, at all "regular communications," the Lodge must invariably be opened on the first, second and third degrees respectively, as explained in the preceding ceremonies, and further that all the ordinary business transactions of the Order, must be conducted in a Lodge of Master Masons only. If it is a special communication, however, and the Lodge is called to work the first degree, it must be opened on that degree; if the second is to be conferred, it must be opened on the first and second; and if the Master Mason's degree is to be conferred, the Lodge must be opened on the first, second and third degrees.

In this exposition, I am supposing that a "regular communication" of the Lodge is held, and that work is to be done on each of the degrees besides; and therefore I shall now explain, first of all, how the ordinary business of a Lodge is usually conducted, and then go on in the regular manner of conferring the degrees. The Lodge being in session, as seen on page 36, the Worshipful Master says:

"Brother Secretary, this being a regular communication, the first business in order will be reading the minutes of our last regular communication."

The Secretary, rising to his feet, then reads the minutes as follows:

Minutes.   Regular communication of Keystone Lodge, No. 639, A. F. & A. M., held in their hall, Nos. 62 & 64, N. Clark St., Chicago, July 2nd, 1873, A. L., 5873.

Officers present.   E. Ronayne, Worshipful Master; Morris Pflaum, Senior Warden; *pro tem.;* Oscar Eckvall, Junior Warden; Fred Becker, Treasurer; Wm. Aiken, Secretary; S. M. Samuelson, Senior Deacon; H. S. Anderson, Junior Deacon; James Anderson, Tyler, *pro tem.*

Members
present.

Visitors
present.

Petitions.

Commit-
tees.

Balloting.

Brothers Prince, Cronin, Loehr, Burkhard, Ross, Morebeck and W. Bro. Dixon.
See Lodge Register, (already alluded
to.)

The Lodge was opened in form on the
first, second and third degrees of Masonry.

The minutes of the last regular communication of June 4th, and of the "special" of June 11th, were read, and declared
approved.

A petition in form was read from Rev.
James Hunt, for initiation. He comes recommended by brothers Ronayne, Dixon
and Prince. The petition was received and
referred to a committee consisting of brothers Anderson, Loehr and Ross.

The committee appointed on the petition of Mr. Nicolaby for initiation, reported favorable; whereupon the committee
was discharged, and ballot ordered.

Also the committee on the application
of Mr. Wood, reported unfavorable; the
report was received, the committee discharged, and ballot ordered.

And the ballot being spread, on the
application of Mr. Nicolaby, and being
found *clear,* he was declared duly elected
to receive the Entered Apprentice degree,
as conferred in this Lodge. The ballot was
also spread on the application of brother
Schriber for advancement to the 2nd degree; and being found clear, he was declared duly elected to receive the Fellow
Craft degree, to be conferred in this Lodge.

The ballot was also spread on the

application of Mr. Wood for the degrees, and being found *not clear,* he was declared rejected.

Commu-
nications.
Communications were read from vari-sister Lodges, announcing the receipt of petitions for degrees and membership; all of which were received and placed on file.

New busi-
ness.
A bill of thirty dollars for rent of hall during the month ending May 31st, was received from Germania Lodge. Also a bill of twenty dollars from Bro. D. Lally, for services as Tyler from March 1st to June 1st, inclusive; both of which were referred to the Finance Committee.

Work.
The Lodge now dispensed with labor on the third degree, and resumed on the first for work; and Mr. Andrew Nicolaby being in waiting, and having satisfactorily answered the usual constitutional questions, he was duly prepared, presented and regularly initiated as an Entered Apprentice. He also received the *benefit* of the lecture, and paid the usual fee of $15. Bro. Schriber, an Entered Apprentice of this Lodge, was then examined in the ritual of that degree, and retired. (See Chapter IV.)

The Lodge now dispensed with *labor* on the first degree, and resumed on the second; and Bro. Schriber being in waiting, was duly prepared, and *passed* to the degree of Fellow Craft. He also received the benefit of a lecture, and paid the usual fee of $15.

The Lodge now dispensed with labor

on the second degree, and resumed on the third; and there being no further business, the Lodge was closed in form on the third, second and first degrees of Masonry.

WILLIAM AIKEN, *Sec'y.*

Receipts: Rev. James Hunt's petition $ 5.00
"   Bro. A. Nicolaby's initiation 15.00
"   Bro. Schriber's second degree 15.00

Total.............................. $35.00

Approved: EDMOND RONAYNE, W. M., Aug. 6th, 1873, A. L., 5873.

Worshipful Master: "Brethren, you have heard the minutes of our 'regular communication' of July 2nd. Are there any alterations or amendments? (He pauses for a few seconds.) If not, they shall be declared approved as read. (Another short pause.) They are so declared, brother Secretary." (One rap.)

SECOND ORDER OF BUSINESS.

Worshipful Master: "Reading and referring petitions: are there any petitions on your table, brother Secretary?"

The Secretary, rising to his feet, says: "I have two petitions, Worshipful" (or one, as the case may be), "as follows:"

FORM OF PETITION.

HALL OF KEYSTONE LODGE, NO. 639, A. F. & A. M.

To the Worshipful Master, Wardens and Brethren of Keystone Lodge, No. 639, A. F. & A. M.:

The petition of the subscriber represents that, having long entertained a favorable opinion of your ancient institution, he is desirous, if found worthy, of being admitted a member thereof; and if admitted, he promises a cheerful compliance with all the ancient usages and customs of the Fraternity. He has not petitioned any other Lodge for the degrees of Masonry.

Recommended by brothers his place of business is 168 Randolph St.
 M. Pflaum, his place of residence is 58 Fourth Ave.
 Benj. F. Prince, his age is 34 years.
 O. Eckvail, His occupation, Merchant.

(Signed)   MORRIS DAVID.

The other is the petition in form of Mr. J. C. Wickers, who comes regularly recommended by Bros. Ronayne, Anderson and Becker; his place of business is corner of Fourth St. and Milwaukee Ave.; occupation, that of a tailor; age 27 years. The usual fee of five dollars accompanies each of these petitions.

Worshipful Master: "Brethren, you have heard the petitions of Mr. Morris David and Mr. Wickers; what is your pleasure with them?"

Bro. Samuelson: "Worshipful Master, I move that the petitions be received, and committees appointed."

Worshipful Master: "If there are no objections, that will be taken as the sense of the Lodge, and I will appoint on the petition of Mr. David, Bros. Cronin, Burkhard and Ross; and on that of Mr. Wickers, Bros. Becker, Loehr and Dixon."

THIRD ORDER OF BUSINESS.

Worshipful Master: "Reports of committee on candidates. Brother Secretary, are there any reports on your desk?"

Secretary: "The committee on the petition of Rev. James Hunt consisting of Bro's Loehr, An-

derson and Ross, have all reported favorable," handing the petition (which must always be in the foregoing form) to the Worshipful Master.

Worshipful Master: "Brethren, you have heard
the report of your committee on the application of
Rev. James Hunt to be made a Mason. What is your
pleasure with it?"

Bro. Becker: "I move that the report be received
the committee discharged, and ballot ordered.

Worshipful Master: "If there are no objections,
that shall be taken as the sense of the Lodge."

FOURTH ORDER OF BUSINESS.

Worshipful Master: "Report of standing committee."

Secretary: "There are none, Worshipful."

FIFTH ORDER OF BUSINESS.

Worshipful Master: "Balloting. Any balloting
on your desk, brother Secretary?"

Secretary: "The ballot is due on the petition
of Mr. Hunt for initiation; and on the application of
Bro. Schriber for advancement to the third degree;
and of Bro. Nicolaby to the second degree.

Worshipful Master: "Brother Senior Deacon,
prepare the ballot box. Brethren, you are now about
to cast your ballot on the petition of Rev. James
Hunt for initiation. He comes recommended by Bro's
Ronayne, Dixon and Prince. The committee, consisting of Bro's Anderson, Loehr and Ross, have all
reported favorable. His Age is forty years; his occupation is minister of the Gospel; his residence is No.
1,091 —— Street. The white ball elects, and the

black rejects. Look well to your ballots, and make no mistake." He drops his ballot into the box.

The Senior Deacon having prepared the ballot box, which is a small box about eight inches long, and five or six inches wide, having two drawers in it,—the front one with a slide in the end of it, which he raises up, exposing to the view the black and white balls mixed, and from which a small hopper leads into the other drawer, through which the ball is passed. He opens the rear drawer (next the handle) which he presents to the Worshipful Master, showing him that it is quite empty, and into which the Worshipful Master drops his ball, through the hopper above described. The Senior Deacon then passes the box around the hall, presenting it to each member, who puts his hand in through the slide, lifts his ball and drops it through the little hopper; and having thus gone the entire round of the Lodge, the Worshipful Master asks: "Have all the brethren voted? If so, I declare the ballot closed. Brother Senior Deacon, you will display the ballot for inspection."—The Senior Deacon now takes the ballot box, first to the Junior Warden in the South, and then to the Senior Warden in the West, each of whom examines the second compartment to see if any black balls are cast; and lastly he presents it to the Worshipful Master who, before he examines it, gives one rap with his gavel, and enquires as follows:

Worshipful Master: "Bro. Junior Warden, how do you find the ballot in the South?"

Junior Warden (there being no black balls): "Clear in the South. Worshipful."

Worshipful Master: "And how in the West, brother Senior Warden?"

Senior Warden: "Clear in the West, Worshipful."

Worshipful Master (examining the ballot box): "And *clear* in the East. I therefore declare Rev. James Hunt duly elected to receive the Entered Apprentice degree, as conferred in this Lodge."

One black ball is enough to cause the rejection of a candidate in any or all of the degrees, or even for membership; and hence, should a black ball appear in the box, of course the response in each case would be, "Not clear," and the Master would declare the candidate rejected. If only one black ball appears another trial is taken.

This is the Illinois method. Another mode of balloting is for the Senior Deacon, after presenting the box to the Worshipful Master, to place it on the altar, and each brother, according to rank, steps in front of the altar and making the due-guard and sign of a Master Mason, deposits his ballot as above described, and retires to his seat. It is a "landmark" that every member present must vote on the admission of a candidate, whether for degrees or membership. And when a candidate is rejected, he cannot apply again for one year, nor can his petition be received in another Lodge without the unanimous consent of the one to which application was first made.

The same routine is gone through with in case of Bro's Schriber and Nicolaby; and no black balls appearing, the former is declared duly elected to receive the third degree, and the latter the second.

SIXTH ORDER OF BUSINESS.

Worshipful Master: "Reading communications. Bro. Secretary, are there any communications on your table?"

The Secretary now reads all communications from sister Lodges, announcing the names of those who have been proposed in each Lodge for initiation or membership since the last regular, and the Worshipful Master enquires:

"Brethren, you have heard the communications from the various sister Lodges. What is your pleasure with them?" (Pausing for a few seconds.). "If there are no objections, they shall be received and placed on file, and the rejections placed on the black list. It is so ordered, brother Secretary."

Should there be any further communications, such as letters or circulars from the Grand Secretary, dispensations from the Grand Master, etc., they are now read and always ordered received and placed on file.

SEVENTH ORDER OF BUSINESS.

Worshipful Master: "Unfinished business?"
Secretary: "There is none, Worshipful."

EIGHTH ORDER OF BUSINESS.

Worshipful Master: "New business?"
Secretary: "There is none."

NINTH ORDER OF BUSINESS.

Worshipful Master: "Work is next in order."

CHAPTER III.

At a regular communication, and when all the ordinary routine business of the Lodge is disposed of the Worshipful Master usually exclaims, as intimated in the last Chapter, "Work is next in order."

Freemasons, we are informed in the text books of the Lodge, are moral builders. It is said of them that, a "more noble and glorious purpose than squaring stones and hewing timbers is theirs,—fitting immortal nature for that spiritual temple—that house not made with hands eternal in the heavens."*

And it is further asserted that, by "speculative Masonry, we are enabled to erect a spiritual temple in the heart, pure and spotless, and fit for the dwelling place of Him who is the Author of purity."†

Now all this being the case, is it not strangely inconsistent and even wicked, on the part of the Masonic fraternity, to exclude from their membership all their own *female* relatives, all their *children,* all old men and women, all deaf, dumb and blind men, all cripples, all colored men, and even all poor men? If Freemasonry teaches me how to erect a spiritual temple in my heart, pure and spotless, why not allow my wife, mother, sister or daughter to engage in the same grand and glorious work? Or why confine the great, moral lessons of the Lodge-room within such narrow limits as those who can pay an immoderately large sum of money for them, and who, besides, are strong, able-bodied men? If Masonry contains anything that would benefit the human family, then the human family ought to know it. If it will make mankind better and nobler, then mankind ought to

---

* Sickle's General Ahiman Rezón, p. 71.
† Mackey's Manual of the Lodge, p. 35.

have the benefit of it. And on the other hand, if it contains anything within itself that is injurious to society; if the principles which it inculcates, and the laws which it enforces, are in direct conflict with the laws of the church, the State and the family; in a word, if Freemasonry is an oath-bound conspiracy of the initiated few against the many; then, most unquestionably, the general public ought to know what it is, and in what that conspiracy consists. If Masonry be a good thing, it must undoubtedly be as good for the multitude,—for all classes and conditions of men and women,—as for the favored few.

For all of these reasons then, I have very great pleasure in now laying before the reader the correct or standard ritual of the system, and so to do what little I can, in bestowing its benefits upon all.

A Masonic degree consists of three general parts, namely; the opening, closing, and initiatory ceremonies; and these three always constitute what is commonly called THE WORK of the Order. This "work," of course, must everywhere be the same in substance, because Masonry is the same everywhere, though now and again a few verbal differences will be found to exist among some Lodges, and even among some Grand Lodges; but these ritualistic differences are so trifling and unimportant in themselves, that a Mason, no matter where he hails from, unless through sheer ignorance or forgetfulness, can always make himself understood.

We shall now go on with our illustrations then, and as already stated, we shall exemplify the "standard ritual and work" of Ancient Craft Masonry, as it is generally accepted and practiced among all the Lodges in the country. *Appendix p. 266.

Supposing that it is a regular communication, and the Lodge being opened on the third degree, it must be *reduced down* to the first for initiation, which is done as follows:

Worshipful Master: "Brother Senior Warden, it is my order that we now dispense with labor on the third degree, and resume on the first for the purpose of work; this you will communicate to the Junior Warden in the South, and he to the brethren, that all having due notice thereof may govern themselves accordingly."

Senior Warden (one rap): "Brother Junior Warden, it is the order of the Worshipful Master that we now dispense with labor on the third degree, and resume on the first for work. This you will communicate to the brethren, that all having due notice thereof may govern themselves accordingly."

Junior Warden (three raps): "Brethren, it is the order of the Worshipful Master, communicated to me by way of the West, that we now dispense with labor on the third degree, and resume on the first for work. Take due notice thereof, and govern yourselves accordingly."

Worshipful Master: "Together, brethren."

All make the due-guard and sign of an Entered Apprentice, as explained on page 16. The Master gives one rap, and the Senior and Junior Wardens also one each, when the Master continues:

Worshipful Master: "Accordingly, I declare Keystone Lodge, No. 639, duly at labor on the first degree of Masonry. Brother Senior Deacon, arrange the altar. Brother Junior Deacon, inform the Tyler."

The Master then gives one rap, and the Lodge is again seated. The Junior Deacon informs the Tyler, as explained already on page 10, and the Senior

Deacon opens the Bible at Psalm 133, and places

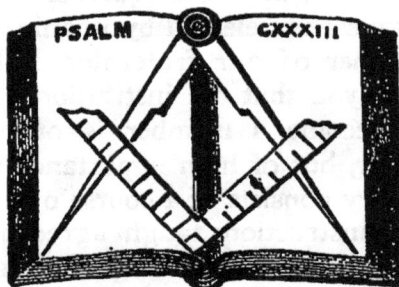

upon it the Square and Compass, with both points below the Square, as in the annexed figure.

INITIATION.

Worshipful Master (one rap) : "Brother Junior Deacon, you will ascertain if there are any candidates in waiting."

Junior Deacon: Repairs to the door and gives three raps.

Tyler: Three raps.

Junior Deacon: "Worshipful Master, Mr. James Hunt is in waiting for the first degree in Masonry."

Worshipful Master: "Brother Secretary, you will take with you the Stewards, retire and propound the usual interrogatories."

Junior Deacon (at the door) : Three raps.

Tyler: Three raps.

(Exit, Secretary and Stewards.)

CHARGE TO CANDIDATES.

Secretary: "Mr. ...., as you have petitioned for initiation into our mysteries, it becomes my duty to propound to you several interrogatories of which I must require of you unequivocal answers.

As you have been elected by unanimous ballot to become a member of our fraternity, it becomes my duty to inform you that the institution of which you are about to become a member is of no light and trifling character, but of high importance and due solemnity. Masonry consists of a course of ancient hieroglyphics, moral instructions taught agreeably to ancient usages by types, emblems and allegorical figures. Even the ceremonies of gaining admission, within these walls are emblematic of events which all mankind must sooner or later experience. They are emblematic at least in some small degree of your great and last change, of your exit from this world, to the world to come. You are undoubtedly aware that whatever man may acquire on earth, whether wealth, honor, titles or even his own merits, can never serve him as a passport to the Grand Lodge above, but previous to his gaining admission there, he must find himself poor and penniless, blind and naked dependent on the will and pleasure of the Supreme Grand Master. He must be divested of the rags of his own righteousness and clothed with a garment from on high. And in order to impress this more deeply on your mind it will be necessary that you be divested of a portion of your outward apparel and clothed in a garment furnished by the Worshipful Master of this Lodge, a garment similar to that worn by all candidates who have gone this way before you.

Are you willing to submit to these rules? (Candidate answer.)

I will then leave you in the hands of true and trusted friends, who will give you the necessary instructions and prepare you in a proper manner for

your initiation as all candidates have been who have gone this way before."

The foregoing questions being thus proposed and answered, the Secretary retires into the Lodge, approaches the altar as usual, makes the due-guard and sign, and reports:

"Worshipful Master, the usual questions have been satisfactorily answered; the first four being answered in the affirmative, and the fifth in the negative; and the usual fee has been collected."

The Junior Deacon then proceeds, with the assistance of the .Stewards, to prepare the candidate for initiation, which is done in the following manner: He is divested of his coat, vest, pants, boots, stockings, drawers, neck tie, collar,—in fact everything except

his shirt. He is then handed a pair of drawers (always furnished by the Lodge.), which he puts on. All

the studs, sleeve-buttons, etc., are taken off his shirt,
and any iron buttons in his inside shirt, are cut out.
Everything of a metallic kind is taken away; the
left leg of the drawers is rolled above the knee, so
as to make the left foot, leg and knee bare; the left
sleeve of his shirt is raised above the elbow, so as to
make the left arm bare and the left breast of the shirt
is tucked back, so as to make his left breast bare. A
slipper is put on his right foot, with the heel slipshod,
a hood-wink is fastened over his eyes, a blue rope,
called a *cable-tow* is put once around his neck, and he
is then *duly* and *truly* prepared to be made a Mason.

The Junior Deacon now leads him to the door
communicating with the Lodge-room, and telling him
to close his fist, takes him by the right hand, and, with
his (candidate's) knuckles, gives three loud and distinct knocks on the door.

Junior Deacon: "Worshipful Master there is an
alarm at the door."

Worshipful Master: "Attend to the alarm, Bro.
Junior Deacon."

Junior Deacon (gives 3 raps): "Tyler informs
Junior Deacon and Junior Deacon reports to the Worshipful Master.

Junior Deacon: "The Secretary desires admission."

Worshipful Master: "You will admit him."

Secretary (at altar makes due-guard and sign):
"Worshipful Master the usual constitutional questions
have been propounded and satisfactorily answered."

Worshipful Master (gives one rap): "Bro. Junior Deacon, you will retire, prepare and present the
candidate for the first degree. Bro. Senior Deacon,
you will attend to all alarms and take charge of the
door.'

Junior Deacon makes due-guard and sign at the altar before going out. Senior Deacon goes directly from his chair to the door and makes alarm to let Junior Deacon out; then takes seat in Junior Deacon's place. Junior Deacon in preparation room gives alarm —three raps on door.

Senior Deacon (rising): "Worshipful Master, there is an alarm at the door of the preparation room."

Worshipful Master: "Brother Senior Deacon, attend to the alarm, and report the cause."

The Senior Deacon with his rod approaches the door, gives three loud and distinct knocks, opens the door and enquires:

Senior Deacon: "Who comes here?"

Junior Deacon: "Rev. James Hunt, who has long been in darkness, and now seeks to be brought to light and to receive a part in the rights and benefits of this Worshipful Lodge, erected to God and dedicated to the Saints John, as all brothers and fellows have done before."

Senior Deacon: "Mr. Hunt, is this of your own free will and accord?"

Mr. Hunt: "It is."

Senior Deacon: "Brother Junior Deacon, is the candidate worthy and well qualified?"

Junior Deacon: "He is."

Senior Deacon: "Is he duly and truly prepared?"

Junior Deacon: "He is."

Senior Deacon: "Is he of lawful age, and properly vouched for?"

Junior Deacon: "He is."

Senior Deacon: "Who vouches for this?"

Junior Deacon: "A brother."

Senior Deacon: "By what further rights and benefits does he expect to gain admission?"

Junior Deacon: "By being a man, free-born, of good report, and well recommended."

Senior Deacon: "It is well, you will wait with patience until the Worshipful Master is informed of your request, and his answer returned."

The door is then closed; the Senior Deacon returns to the altar, gives three raps on the floor with his rod, and reports :*

Senior Deacon: "Worshipful Master, the alarm was caused by Rev. James Hunt, who has long been in darkness, and now seeks to be brought to light and to receive a part in the rights and benefits of this Worshipful Lodge, erected to God, and dedicated to the Saints John, as all brothers and fellows have done before."

Worshipful Master: "Brother Senior Deacon, is this of his own free will and accord?"

Senior Deacon: "It is."

Worshipful Master: "Is the candidate worthy and well qualified?"

Senior Deacon: "He is."

Worshipful Master: "Is he duly and truly prepared?"

Senior Deacon: "He is."

Worshipful Master: "Is he of lawful age, and properly vouched for?"

Senior Deacon: "He is."

Worshipful Master: "Who vouches for this?"

Senior Deacon: "A brother."

Worshipful Master: "By what further rights and benefits does he expect to gain admission?"

Senior Deacon: "By being a man, free born, of good report, and well recommended."

---

* For the preparation ceremonies, see "Master's Carpet," pp. 253-260.

Worshipful Master: "It is well. Since he comes endowed with all these necessary qualifications, it is my order that he enter this Lodge in the name of the Lord, and be received in due form."

RITE OF INDUCTION.

The Senior Deacon returns to the door, which he immediately opens, and says: "It is the order of the Worshipful Master that the candidate enter this Lodge in the name of the Lord, and be received in due form." The candidate is then conducted into the Lodge-room, and halted about six or eight feet from the door, where the Senior Deacon receives him on the point of the Compass, pressed to his naked left breast, and addressing him in the following words, performs the "Shock of Entrance," or the "Rite of Induction," as represented in the figure.*

* For the origin of this ceremony see "Master's Carpet," pp. 295-267.

Senior Deacon: "Mr. Hunt, upon your first admission into a Lodge of Masons, I receive you upon the point of a sharp instrument pressing your naked left breast (here he presses the point of the Compass against the left breast of the candidate), which is to teach you that, as this is an instrument of torture to your flesh, so should the recollection of it be to your conscience, should you ever presume to reveal any of the secrets of Freemasonry unlawfully."

The Senior Deacon then passes the Compass to the Steward, and taking the candidate by the right arm, conducts him a little further inward, and towards the center of the Lodge, where he is halted, the Junior Deacon in the meantime, retiring to his proper place, and the Stewards marching behind the candidate. The Senior Deacon then addresses the latter as follows:

"No man should ever enter upon any great or important undertaking, without first invoking the blessing of Deity, you will therefore kneel and attend prayer."

The figure on the next page is a correct representation of the Lodge and candidate during this ceremony.

The Master then gives three raps, removes his hat, and repeats the following

PRAYER

"Vouchsate thine aid, Almighty Father of the universe, to this, our present convention, and grant that this candidate for Masonry may so dedicate and devote his life to Thy service, that he may become a true and faithful brother among us. Endue him with a competency of Thy divine wisdom, that by the influence of the pure principles of our Order, he may be better enabled to display the beauties of Brotherly

Love, Relief and Truth, to the honor of Thy holy name. Amen.''

Candidate kneeling in Mock Worship.

Brethren respond, "So mote it be."

The Master, then resuming his hat, approaches the candidate, still kneeling, and placing his right hand upon his head, as represented on the next page, demands:

Worshipful Master: "Mr. Hunt, in whom do you put your trust?"

Candidate: "In God."

Worshipful Master: "Give me your right hand. Your trust being in God your faith is well founded. Arise! follow your conductor, and fear no danger."

*Cook's Standard Monitor, 1903, p. 9.

(Helping the candidate to his feet.)   The Master then
retires to his seat in the East, gives one rap, and the
Lodge is seated.

RITE OF CIRCUMAMBULATION.

The Senior Deacon again taking the candidate
by the right arm, as represented in the annexed figure,
next page, conducts him slowly once around the Lodge-
room, and as they pass the stations of the Master and
Wardens, each of these officers gives one loud rap with
his gavel,—the Junior Warden giving the first one,—

and the candidate being blindfolded, these raps often startle him considerably.

The following Psalm is also read or repeated while he is being led around, and the reading is so timed that it is finished just as the Deacon and candidate, having made one circuit of the Lodge, arrive at the Junior Warden's station:

"Behold how good and how pleasant it is for brethren to dwell together in unity. It is like the precious ointment upon the head, that ran down upon the beard,—even unto Aaron's beard,—that went down to the skirts of his garments, as the dew of Hermon, and as the dew that descended upon the mountains of Zion; for there the Lord commanded his blessing, even life forevermore."*

On the next page is correctly represented the journey of the candidate around the Lodge in the Entered

* "Standard Monitor." Cook. 1903.

EAST.

TYLAR.
*

SECY.
*

S. D.
*

W. M.

SOUTH.
J. W.

A

B

S. W.   J. D.

WEST.

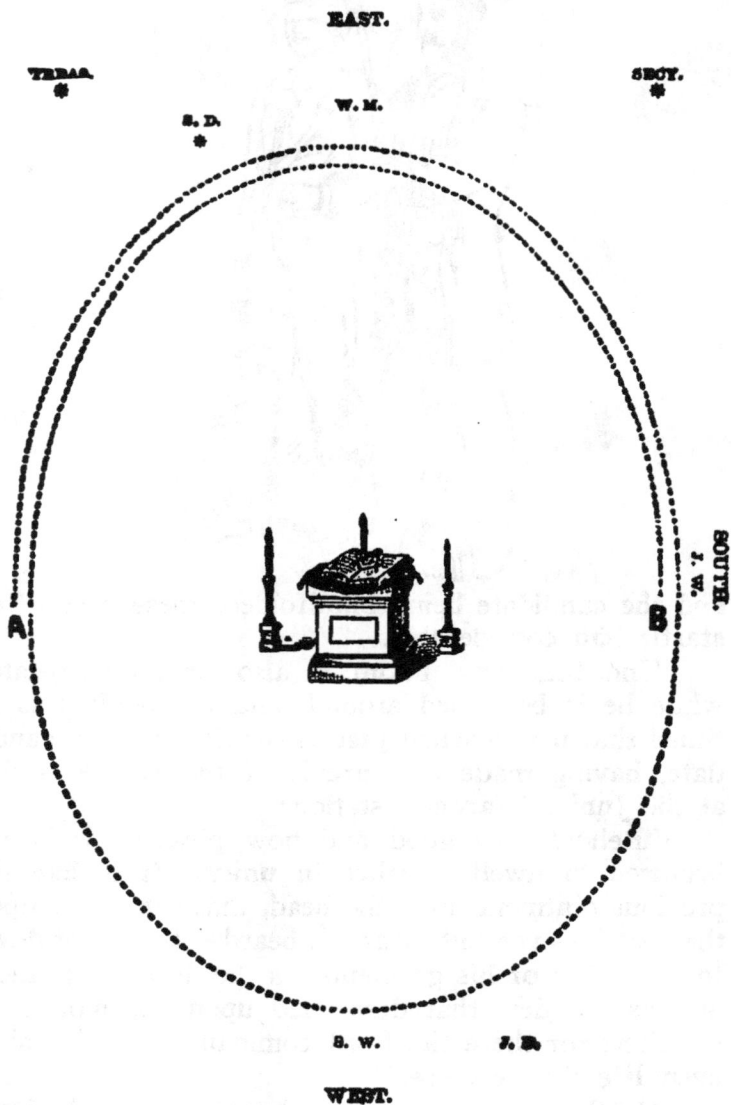

RITE OF CIRCUMAMBULATION.

Apprentice degree. Starting at the point A, where he has been kneeling for a mock prayer, the Senior Deacon conducts him around by way of the East to the South, thence to the West, and so by way of the East to the South again, stopping at the point B.*

Having arrived at the South, the Deacon gives one rap with his rod on the floor, and the Junior Warden, rising to his feet, demands:

Junior Warden: "Who comes here?"

Senior Deacon: "Dr. James Hunt, who has long been in darkness, and now seeks to be brought to light, and to receive a part in the rights and benefits of this Worshipful Lodge, erected to God and dedicated to the Saints John, as all brothers and fellows have done before."

Junior Warden: "Dr. Hunt, is this of your own free will and accord?"

Candidate: "It is."

Junior Warden: "Bro. Senior Deacon, is the candidate worthy and well qualified?"

Senior Deacon: "He is."

Junior Deacon: "Is he duly and truly prepared?"

Senior Deacon: "He is."

Junior Deacon: "Is he of lawful age, and properly vouched for?"

Senior Deacon: "He is."

Junior Deacon: "Who vouches fo this?"

Senior Deacon: "A brother."

Junior Deacon: "By what further rights and benefits does he expect to gain this favor?"

Senior Deacon: "By being a man, free born, of good report, and well recommended."

Junior Warden: "It is well. You will con-

*For the origin of this rite, see "Master's Carpet," pp. 269-272.

duct the candidate to the Senior Warden in the West for further examination."

He is now conducted to the West, and the Senior Deacon again giving three raps with his rod, the Senior Warden rises, gives one rap, and the very same questions are asked, and like answers returned, as at the South, after which, the Senior Warden replies:

Senior Warden: "It is well.—You will conduct the candidate to the Worshipful Master in the East for further examination."

Being led to the East, the Deacon again raps one, and the Master, without rising, demands:

Worshipful Master: "Who comes here?"

Senior Deacon: "Rev. Dr. James Hunt, who has long been in darkness, and now seeks to be brought to light, and to receive a part in the rights and benefits of this Worshipful Lodge, erected to God and dedicated to the Saints John, as all brothers and fellows have done before."

Worshipful Master: "Mr. Hunt, is this of your own free will and accord?"

Candidate: "It is."

Worshipful Master: "Brother Senior Deacon, is the candidate worthy and well qualified?"

Senior Deacon: "He is."

Worshipful Master: "Is he duly and truly prepared?"

Senior Deacon: "He is."

Worshipful Master: "Is he of lawful age, and properly vouched for?"

Senior Deacon: "He is."

Worshipful Master: "Who vouches for this?"

Senior Deacon: "A brother."

Worshipful Master: "By what further rights and benefits does he expec to *gain this favor?*"

Senior Deacon: "By being a man, free born, of good report, and well recommended."

Worshipful Master: "It is well. Since he comes endowed with all these necessary qualifications, it is my order that you re-conduct him to the Senior Warden in the West, who will teach him how to approach the East by *one* upright, regular step, his feet forming the angle of a square, his body erect, at the altar before the Worshipful Master."

The candidate is re-conducted to the Senior Warden, as directed, being led by way of the South, and halted about five feet from that officer's station, where the following ceremony occurs:

Senior Deacon: "Brother Senior Warden, it is the order of the Worshipful Master that you teach the candidate to approach the East by one upright, regular step, his feet forming the angle of a square, his body erect, at the altar before the Worshipful Master."

Senior Warden: "Brother Senior Deacon, you will face the candidate to the East. (The candidate is faced about.) Mr. Hunt, you will step off one step with your left foot, bringing the heel of the right to the hollow of the left, forming the angle of a square. Stand erect. (The Senior Deacon places his feet as required.) Stand erect.—In order, Worshipful." (See Fig. on page 68.)

The Master then rises to his feet, and addresses the candidate as follows:

Worshipful Master (gives three raps): "Mr. Hunt, you are now at the *altar* of Masonry for the first time; but before proceeding further in our solemn ceremonies, it becomes my duty, as Worshipful Master of this Lodge, to inform you that, it will be necessary that you take upon yourself the solemn oath or obligation pertaining to this degree. And I can as

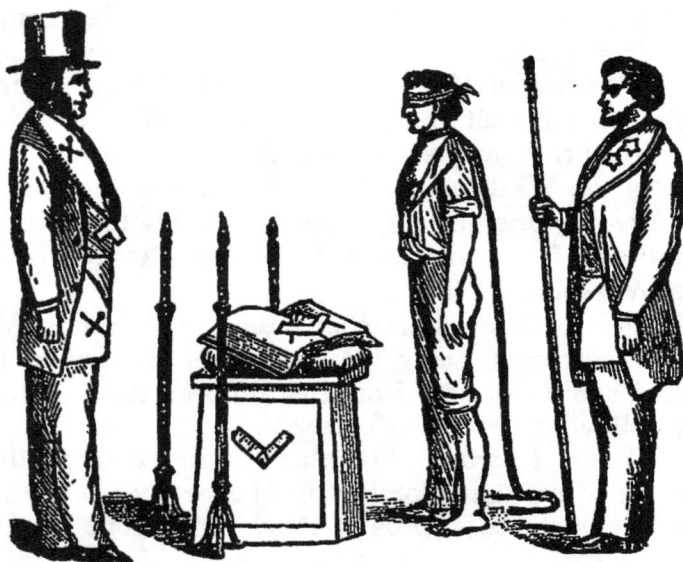

Worshipful Master.   Candidate.   Senior Deacon

sure you upon the honor of a man and a Mason, that
in this obligation there is nothing that will conflict with
any duty you owe to God, your country, your family,
your neighbor, or yourself. In your advancement
thus far, you have repeatedly assured us, it was of
your own free will and accord. If you are still of the
same mind, you will advance to our altar. (He is
led to the altar by his guide, the Senior Deacon.)
Kneel upon your naked left knee, your right (knee)
forming a square, your left hand supporting the Holy
Bible, Square and Compasses, your right resting thereon (the Senior Deacon places the candidate in these
different positions), in which due form you will say
 'I,' repeat your name and say after me

RITE OF SECRECY.*

At the word "thereon," the Master gives three raps, calling all the brethren to their feet, who arrange themselves in two rows, on either side of the altar, from East to West; he then approaches the altar, removes his hat, and administers the following obligation in mock solemnity, the candidate repeating after the Master:

Candidate being made a Mason.

ENTERED APPRENTICE OBLIGATION.

"I, James Hunt, of my own free will and accord, in the presence of Almighty God and this Worshipful Lodge, erected to Him and dedicated to the Saints John, do hereby and hereon (here the Master places his right hand on that of the candidate), most solemnly and sincerely promise and swear, that I will always

*For the origin of this rite, see "Master's Carpet," pp 273-278.

hail, ever conceal and never reveal any of the secret arts, parts or points of the hidden mysteries of Ancient Freemasonry, which have been heretofore, may at this time, or shall at any future period, be communicated to me as such, to any person or persons whomsoever, except it be to a true and lawful brother of this degree, or within a regularly constituted Lodge of Masons, and neither unto him nor them, until by strict trial, due examination, or legal information, I shall have found him or them as lawfully entitled to the same as I am myself.

"I furthermore promise and swear that I will not write, print, paint, stamp, stain, cut, carve, mark nor engrave them, nor cause the same to be done upon anything movable or immovable, capable of receiving the least impression of a word, syllable, letter or character, whereby the same may become legible or intelligible to any person under the canopy of heaven.

"All this I most solemnly and sincerely promise and swear, with a firm and steadfast resolution, to keep and perform the same without any equivocation, mental reservation or secret evasion of mind whatever, binding myself under a no less penalty than that of having my throat cut across, my tongue torn out by its roots and buried in the rough sands of the sea at low water mark, where the tide ebbs and flows twice in twenty-four hours, should I ever knowingly violate this my solemn obligation of an Entered Apprentice Mason. So help me God, and keep me steadfast in the due performance of the same."

"In token of your sincerity, you will detach your hands and kiss the Bible."

The Deacon removes the candidate's hands, and he kisses the Bible.

Worshipful Master: "Brother Senior Deacon.

you will release the brother from the cable-tow, he is bound to us by an obligation,- a tie stronger than human hands can impose."

The Senior Deacon removes the rope from around the candidate's neck, and throws it aside. The Master resumes his hat, steps back a few paces, and asks the candidate:

Worshipful Master: "Bro. Hunt, in your present condition, what do you most desire?"

Candidate (prompted by Senior Deacon): "Light."

Worshipful Master: "Brother Senior Deacon and brethren, you will assist me in bringing this brother from darkness to light."

RITE OF ILLUMINATION.*

Here all the brethren assemble around the altar, and place themselves in two rows, extending from the altar towards the East, as already indicated, the Stewards with their rods standing one at the end of each row, and having their rods crossed over the Master's head. All being thus arranged, the Master goes on:

Worshipful Master: "In the beginning, God created the heaven and the earth. And the earth was without form, and void, and darkness was upon the face of the deep; and the Spirit of God moved upon the face of the waters. And God said, 'Let there be light,' and there was light. In humble commemoration of which august event, we masonically say, 'Let there be light,' and there is light."

Here the hoodwink is quickly removed by the Senior Deacon, who stands behind the candidate, and

---

* For the origin of this rite, see "Master's Carpet," pp. 281-
284

Candidate being brought to light.

the Master and all the brethren make the due-guard
of an Entered Apprentice, as in the figure.* Standing
thus for a little while, the Master concludes. Then all
drop their hands again.

Worshipful Master (approaching the altar) : "My
brother, upon being brought to light in this degree, you
discover the THREE GREAT LIGHTS in Masonry,
by the assistance of the three lesser. The three great
lights in Masonry are the HOLY BIBLE, SQUARE
and COMPASS. The Bible is given as the rule and
guide of our faith; the Square, to square our actions;
and the Compass to circumscribe and keep us within
due bounds.* The three lesser lights are three burning tapers, placed in a triangular form, representing

___

*In some Lodges they stamp on. the floor with the right
foot, and strike the palm of the right hand against the left.
*App. Note A., p. 266.
*"Standard Monitor," Cook, 1903, p. 10.

the sun, moon, and Master of the Lodge, and are thus explained: As the sun rules the day, and the moon governs the night, so should the Worshipful Master endeavor to rule and govern his Lodge with equal regularity."

RITE OF ENTRUSTING.*

The Master then steps back a few paces and facing the altar, makes the due guard and sign of an Entered Apprentice; the Senior Deacon at the same time, addressing the candidate, says:

"Brother Hunt, you now behold the Worshipful Master approaching you from the East, under the dueguard and sign of an Entered Apprentice Mason."

Worshipful Master: "An Entered Apprentice steps off with his left foot (again making the step,) bringing the heel of the right to the hollow of the left, forming the angle of a square, and this is the first step in Masonry. This is the due-guard (makes the due-guard; see page 26), of an Entered Apprentice and alludes to the position in which your hands were placed while taking your obligation. This is the sign (makes the penal sign; see page 27), of an Entered Apprentice, and alludes to the penalty of your obligation."

The Master then approaches the altar, and continues:

Worshipful Master: "In token of friendship and brotherly love, I present you my right hand, and with it the *grip* and *word* of an Entered Apprentice; but as you are uninstructed, I will explain them with Brother Senior Deacon."

Worshipful Master (taking the candidate by the right hand): "Brother Senior Deacon, I hail."

---

*For the origin of this rite, see "Master's Carpet," pp. 287-292.

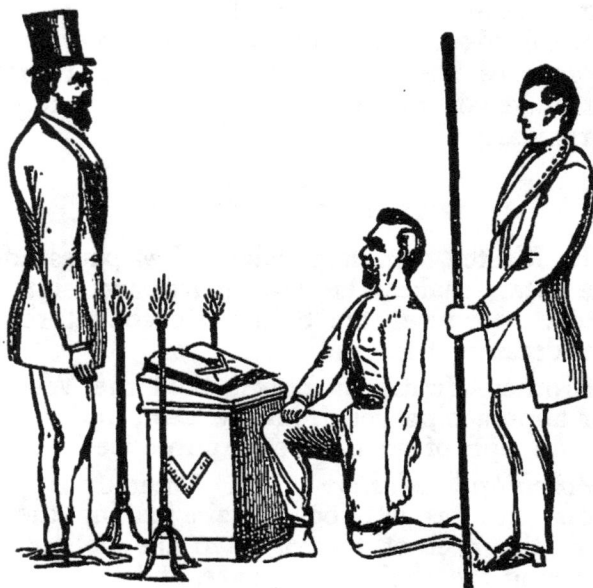

Senior Deacon: "I conceal."
Worshipful Master: "What do you conceal?"
Senior Deacon: "All the secrets of Masons in Masonry, to which this token alludes. (At the word "token" the Senior Deacon presses the top of the candidate's thumb against the first knuckle-joint of the Master's first finger, the Master also pressing his thumb against the candidate's knuckle. See Fig.)

Worshipful Master: "What is this?"
Senior Deacon: "A grip."
Worshipful Master: "Of what?"
Senior Deacon: "Of an Entered Apprentice Mason."

Worshipful Master: "Has it a name?"

Senior Deacon: "It has."

Worshipful Master: "Will you give it to me?"

Senior Deacon: "I did not so receive it, neither will I so impart it."

Worshipful Master: "How will you dispose of it?"

Senior Deacon: "I will letter and halve it with you."

Worshipful Master: "Letter and begin."

Senior Deacon: "No you begin."

Worshipful Master: "You must begin."

Senior Deacon: "A."

Worshipful Master: "Z."

Senior Deacon: "AZ."

Worshipful Master: "B."

Senior Deacon: "O."

Worshipful Master: "BO."

Senior Deacon: "Boaz."

Worshipful Master (to the candidate): "The grip is right, the word is right. You will now arise and salute the Junior and Senior Wardens as an Entered Apprentice."

The candidate is here assisted to his feet, the Master retires to his seat raps the Lodge down, the candidate is conducted by the Senior Deacon to the Junior and Senior Wardens, before each of whom he makes the *step,* due-guard and sign, and is led towards the East, halting on a line with the altar.

Worshipful Master (one rap): "How is it in the South, brother Junior Warden?"

Junior Warden (rising, and making the due-guard): "All right in the South, Worshipful."

Worshipful Master (one rap): "How is it in the West brother Senior Warden?"

Senior Warden (rising and making the due-guard): "All right in the West, Worshipful."

The Master now takes a white leather apron and approaches the candidate, saying:

RITE OF INVESTITURE.*

Worshipful Master (one rap): "My brother, I now have the pleasure of presenting you with a lamb-skin, or white leather apron. It is an emblem of innocence and the badge of a Mason. More ancient than the Golden Fleece or Roman Eagle, more honorable than the Star and Garter, or any other order that can be

conferred upon you at this time or at any future period, by king, prince, potentate or any other person, except he be a Mason; and which I hope you will wear with equal pleasure to yourself and honor to the Fraternity. You will carry it to the Senior Warden

*For the origin of this rite, see "Master's Carpet," pp. 292-296.

in the West, who will teach you how to wear it as an Entered Apprentice."*

The candidate should here be re-conducted to the West, without passing around the altar; and the Senior Deacon, giving one rap, addresses the Senior Warden as follows:

Senior Deacon: "Brother Senior Warden, it is the order of the Worshipful Master that you teach the brother how to wear his apron as an Entered Apprentice."

The Senior Warden, taking the apron from the candidate, unfolds it, and while tying it on, says:

Senior Warden: "My brother, Masonic tradition informs us that at the building of King Solomon's Temple, there were three principal classes of workmen, each of whom, as a distinctive badge, wore their aprons in a particular manner. Entered Apprentices, being bearers of burden, wore theirs with the bib turned up to prevent soiling their clothing; and although spots upon the apron of the operative workman brought credit, rather than disgrace, yet, you as a speculative Mason, are taught to keep yours unspotted from the world."

The candidate is then conducted in front of the Worshipful Master in the East, who rises from his seat, and addresses him as follows:

Worshipful Master: "My brother, it now becomes my duty in accordance with an ancient custom adopted in every regular and well governed lodge to request you to deposit something of a metallic kind, not for its intrinsic worth, but that it may be laid up among the records in the archives of the Lodge as a memorial that you were here made a Mason. I there-

---

*"Standard Monitor," Cook, 1903, p. 11.

fore make this request of you, something of a metalic kind.

This proceeding often embarrasses the candidate very much, especially if he has not read Masonic expositions, for having left all his clothing, money, etc., in the preparation room, he is not at all in a fit condition to respond to a request for a deposit of money or anything else of a metalic kind, to be laid up in the archives of the Lodge or elsewhere.

Worshipful Master: "My brother, you are poor indeed, this request has not been made to trifle with your feelings, as we well know, if you were duly and truly prepared you had nothing of a metalic kind about you, but it is to make a deep and lasting impression on your mind and should you ever meet a friend more especially a brother Mason in a like destitute situation you should contribute as liberally to his relief as your ability will permit without material injury to yourself."

Senior Deacon then places candidate in the North-East corner of Lodge, "his feet forming the angle of a square,"—that is, on the step of an Entered Apprentice,—and his body erect, where the Worshipful Master gives him the following charge and performs what is called "the North-East corner ceremony."

Worshipful Master: "My brother, you now stand in the North-East corner of the Lodge as the youngest Entered Apprentice, and it is with pleasure I can say that you there stand as a just and upright Mason and I give it you strictly in charge ever to walk and act as such.

"As you are now clothed as an Entered Apprentice, you are entitled to your working tools.

THE WORKING TOOLS

of an Entered Apprentice are the twenty-four **inch
gauge** and the common gavel." (The Master, holding
these implements in his hand, presents them to the
candidate.)

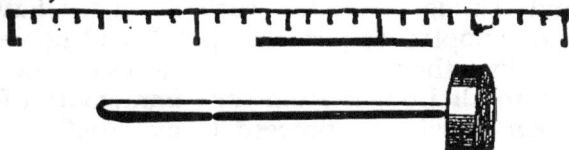

"The twenty-four inch gauge is an instrument
made use of by operative Masons to measure and lay
out their work; but we, as Free and Accepted Masons,
are taught to make use of it for the more noble and
glorious purpose of dividing our time. It being divided into twenty-four equal parts, is emblematical of
the twenty-four hours of the day, which we are taught
to divide into three equal parts, whereby we find
eight hours for the service of God, and a distressed
worthy brother, eight for our usual vocations, and
eight for refreshment and sleep."

"The common gavel is an instrument made use of
by operative Masons to break off the rough and super-
fluous parts of stones, the better to fit them for the
builder's use; but we, as Free and Accepted Masons,
are taught to make use of it for the more noble and
glorious purpose of divesting our hearts and consciences of the vices and superfluities of life, thereby
fitting our minds as living stones, for that spiritual
building,—that house not made with hands,—eternal
in the heavens.* You will now be reconducted to the
place whence you came, invested with what you have
been divested of and returned to the Lodge for further instruction."

* "Standard Monitor." Cook. 1903. p. 18.

SECOND SECTION.

Worshipful Master: "My brother, you have now passed through the forms and ceremonies of your initiation, many of which to you may have appeared of a light and trifling character, such as might have been waived or adopted at pleasure, but I will however inform you that they are such as have been adopted and practiced in all Lodges from time immemorial for reasons which I will now proceed to explain."

"You were divested *of all metals* when prepared to be made a Mason for two reasons,—first, that you might carry nothing offensive or defensive into the Lodge; and secondly, at the building of King Solomon's Temple, there was not heard the sound of ax, hammer, or any tool of iron. The stones were all hewn, squared, and numbered in the quarries where they were raised; the timber felled and prepared in the forests of Lebanon, conveyed by sea in floats to Joppa, and thence by land to Jerusalem, where they were set up by wooden mauls prepared for that purpose; the building, when completed (its several parts fitting with such exactness), had more the appearance of the handy workmanship of the Supreme Architect of the universe, than of human hands. (See p. 54.)

"You were *neither naked nor clad,* because Masonry regards no man for his worldly wealth or honors; this therefore was to signify that it is the internal, and not the external qualifications of a man that should recommend him to be made a Mason. (p. 55.)

"You were *neither barefoot nor shod,* this was in conformity to an ancient Israelitish custom. We read in the book of Ruth of the manner in former times

concerning redeeming and concerning changing; then
to conform all things, a man plucked off his shoe and
gave it to his neighbor; and this was a testimony in
Israel. This, therefore, was to signify the sincerity of
your intentions in the business upon which you were
about to enter.` (p. 55.)

"You were *hoodwinked and with a cable-tow once
around your neck,* for three reasons; first, that as you
were then in darkness, so should you keep all the world
as regards the secrets of Freemasonry, until they shall
obtain them as lawfully as you were then about to do;
secondly, that your hearts may be taught to conceive,
before your eyes, behold the beauties of Freemasonry;
thirdly, had you refused to submit to the forms and
ceremonies of your initiation, being found unworthy to
be taken by the hand as a brother, you might, by the
help of a cable-tow have been led . out of the Lodge
without discovering even the form thereof. (p. 55.)

"You were caused to *give hree distinct knocks,*
to alarm the Lodge, and inform the Worshipful Master that you were prepared for initiation, and these
allude to a text in Scripture: 'Ask, and it shall be
given unto you; seek, and you shall find; knock, and
it shall be opened unto you;' you might have applied
this to your then situation in Masonry in this manner, You *asked* the recommendation of a friend to
be made a Mason; through his recommendation, you
sought initiation; you *knocked* at the door of the
Lodge, and it was opened unto you. (p. 55.)

"You were *received on the point of a sharp instrument, pressing your naked left breast,* to signify
that, as that was an instrument of torture to your
flesh, so should the recollection of it be to your conscience, should you ever presume to reveal any of the
secrets of Freemasonry unlawfully. (p. 59.)

"You were *conducted to the center of the Lodge, caused to kneel and attend prayer,* because no man should ever enter upon any great or important underaking, without first invoking the blessing of Deity. (p. 61.)

"You were *asked in whom you put your trust,* because, according to our Masonic Institution, no atheist can be made a Mason. It was therefore necessary that you should profess your belief in Deity, otherwise no oath or obligation would have been considered binding upon you. (p. 62.)

"You were *taken by the right hand, ordered to arise, follow your conductor and fear no danger,* to signify that, at a time when you could neither foresee nor avoid danger, you were in the hands of a true and trusty friend; in whose fidelity you might with safety confide. (p. 63.)

"You were *conducted once around the Lodge,* that all the brethren might see that you were duly and truly prepared. (p. 64.)

"You were caused to meet with several obstructions on your passage around the Lodge, because there were guards placed at the South, West, and East gates of the outer court of King Solomon's Temple, to see that none passed or repassed, but such as were duly qualified and had permission. It was therefore necessary that you should meet with these several obstructions that vou might be duly examined before you could be made a Mason.

"You were *caused to kneel upon your naked left knee,* because the left has ever been considered the weaker part of man; this therefore was to signify that it was the weaker part of Masonry upon which you were about to enter, being that of an Entered Apprentice. (p. 69.)

"You were caused to lay your right hand on the Holy Bible, Square and Compass, because the right hand, has in all ages been deemed the seat of *fidelity;* the ancients at times worshipped a Deity under the name of *Fides,* which we sometimes see represented by two right hands joined; at others, by two human figures holding each other by the right hand. (p. 69.) The right hand therefore was made use of on this occasion to testify in the strongest manner possible, the sincerity of your intention in the business in which you were then engaged.*

"You were *presented with a lambskin, or white leather apron,* because the lamb has in all ages been deemed an emblem of innocence. He, therefore, who wears the lambskin or white leather apron as the badge of a Mason, is thereby continually reminded of that purity of life and conduct which is so essentially necessary to his gaining admission into the celestial Lodge above, where the Supreme Architect of the universe presides. (p. 76.)*

"You were requested to deposit something of a metalic kind to remind you of your then extremely poor and penniless condition, and should you ever meet

* "Standard Monitor," Cook, 1903, p. 13.

a friend more especially a brother Mason, in a like destitute situation, you should contribute as liberally to his relief as your ability will permit without material injury to yourself. (p. 78.)

"You were placed in the North-East corner of the Lodge as the youngest Entered Apprentice, in operative Masonry, the first stone of a building is usually laid in the North-East corner; you were therefore there placed to receive your first instruction, whereon to build your future moral and Masonic edifice. (p. 78.)

"And lastly, you were presented with the working tools, and taught their uses."   (p. 79.)

THIRD SECTION.

"I will now proceed to explain to you what constitutes a Lodge, its *form, supports, covering, furniture, ornaments, lights, jewels; how situated, and to whom dedicated.**

"A Lodge consists of a number of Free and Accepted Masons duly assembled with the Holy Bible, Square and Compass, and a Charter or Warrant empowering them to work.**

"Our ancient brethren met on high hills or low vales, the better to guard against the approach of cowans and eavesdroppers ascending or descending.

*For the origin of all these emblems, see "Master's Carpet," pp. 298-315.
**"Standard Monitor," Cook, 1903, p. 19.

"The form of a Lodge is an oblong rectangle extending from East to West between North and South,
forming the earth, Heavens and from the. surface

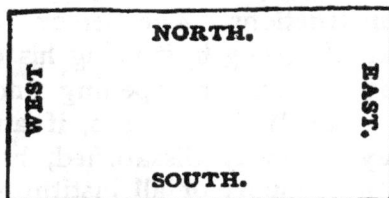

to the center. .It is said to be thus extensive, that denotes the universality of Masonry and that as Masons,
Christians should be equally extensive.

"*Supports:* Masonry may be said to be meta-
phorically supported by three great pillars called Wis-

dom, Strength and Beauty; because, it is necessary
that there should be *wisdom* to contrive, *strength* to
support, and *beauty* to· adorn all great and important
undertakings. They are represented by the three principal officers of the Lodge, Worshipful Master, Senior
and Junior Wardens.*

*App. note B., page 266.

"The Worshipful Master represents the pillar of wisdom, it being supposed that he has wisdom to open and govern his Lodge, set the Craft to work and give them proper instructions. The Senior Warden represents the pillar of strength, it being his duty to assist the Worshipful Master in opening and closing his Lodge, pay the Craft their wages, if any be due, so that none may go away dissatisfied, harmony being the strength and support of all institutions, especially ours.   The Junior Warden represents the pillar of beauty, it being his duty to observe the sun at meridian height, the beauty and glory of the day.

"*Covering:* The *covering* of a Lodge is the clouded canopy, or starry decked heaven, where all good Masons hope at last, to arrive by the aid of a

ladder called Jacob's Ladder having three principal rounds denominated *faith, hope* and *charity,* teaching *faith* in God, *hope* in immortality, and *charity* to all mankind.   But the greatest of these is *charity;* for faith may be lost in sight, hope ends in fruition, but charity extends beyond the grave to the boundless realms of eternity.

"*Furniture:* The *furniture* of a Lodge is the Holy Bible, Square and Compasses. The Bible* we dedicate to the service of God, the Square to the Mas-

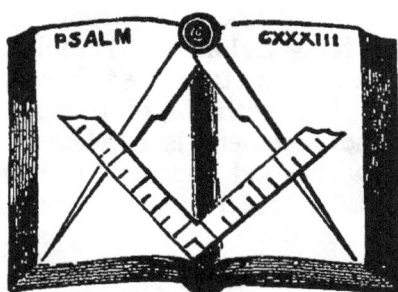

ter, and the Compasses to the Craft. The Bible we dedicate to the service of God because it is His inestimable gift to man *and on it we obligate a newly admitted brother.* The Square to the Master because it is the proper Masonic emblem of his offices and by it he is constantly reminded of the duty he owes to the Lodge over which he has been called to preside and the Compasses to the Craft who by due attention to their use are taught to circumscribe their desires and keep their passions within due bounds with all mankind but more especially with our Brethren in Freemasonry.

"*Ornaments:* The *ornaments* of a Lodge are the Mosaic pavement, the indented tessel, and the blazing

star. The Mosaic pavement is a representation of the ground floor of King Solomon s Temple; the indented tessel, of that beautiful tesselated border or skirting which surrounded it, with the blazing star in the center. The Mosaic pavement is emblematical of human life, checkered with good and evil; the indented tessel which surrounds it, of those manifold blessings and comforts which surround us in this life, and which we hope to enjoy by a faithful reliance on Divine Providence, which is hieroglyphically represented by the blazing star in the center.

"*Lights:* A Lodge has three lights* situated in the East, West, and South, there is none in the North, because of the situation of King Solomon's Temple, which was placed so far North of the ecliptic

that neither sun nor moon at meridian height could dart any rays into the North portion thereof (?) The North therefore, we Masonically term a place of darkness.

"*Jewels:* A Lodge has six *jewels,* three im-

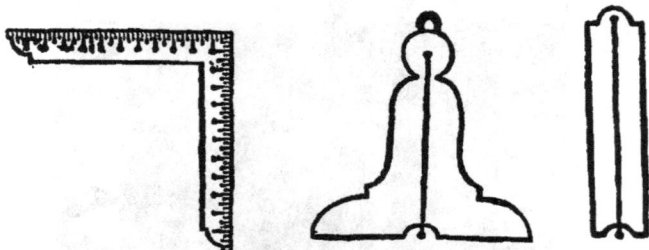

*"Standard Monitor," Cook, p. 16.
*App. note D., page 267.

movable and three movable. The immovable jewels are the Square, Level and Plumb. The Square teaches morality; the Level, equality; and the Plumb, rectitude of life, and are worn by the three principal officers of the Lodge, the Worshipful Master, Senior and Junior Wardens. The movable jewels are the *rough ashler, perfect ashler, and trestle-board.*

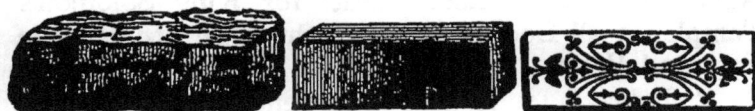

"The *rough ashler* is a stone taken from the quarry in its rude and natural state. The *perfect ashler* is a stone, made ready by the hands of the workmen to be adjusted by the working tools of the Fellow Craft. The trestle-board is for the Master to draw his designs upon. By the rough ashler, we are reminded of our rude and imperfect state by nature; by the perfect ashler, of that state of perfection at which we hope to arrive by a virtuous education, our own endeavors and the blessing of God; and by the trestle-board, we are also reminded that as the operative workman erects his temporal building agreeably to the rules and designs laid down by the Master on his trestle board, so should we both, operative and speculative, endeavor to erect our spiritual building agreeably to the rules and designs laid down by the Supreme Architect of the universe in the great books of nature and revelation, which are our spiritual, moral and Masonic trestle-board.

"*Situation:* *Lodges are situated due East, and West, because King Solomon's Temple was so situated. King Solomon's Temple was so situated because

*App. note E., page 267.

Moses after safely conducting the children of Israe
through the Red sea, when pursued by Pharoah and
his hosts, had erected by divine command, a tabernacle
dedicated to God, which was placed due East and
West to perpetuate the remembrance of that mighty
East wind by which their miraculous deliverance was
wrought and to receive the rays of the rising sun. This
tabernacle was an exact model for King Solomon's
Temple, so all Lodges are or ought to be situated due
East and West.

"*Dedication:* Lodges in ancient times were dedicated to King Solomon, he being our first Most Excellent Grand Master, in modern times, to St. John,
the Baptist, and St. John, the Evangelist—two eminent
Christian patrons of Freemasonry; and since their
time, there has been represented in every regular and
well furnished Lodge a Certain Point within a Circle
embordered by two perpendicular parallel lines representing St. John, the Baptist, and St. John, the Evangelist. On the top of the Circle rests the Book of
Holy Scriptures; the point represents an individual
Brother, the Circle the boundary line of his duty.

In going around this circle, we necessarily touch
on the two parallel lines, as well as on the Book of
Holy Scriptures; and while a Mason keeps himself
circumscribed within their precepts it is impossible that
he should materially err.

BROTHERLY LOVE, RELIEF AND TRUTH.

"The tenets of a Mason's profession are *brotherly
love, relief and truth.* By the exercise of *brotherly
love,* we are taught to regard the whole human species
as one family,—the high, and low, rich, and poor,—

* "Standard Monitor." Cook. 1903. pp. 18. 19.

who, as created by one Almighty Parent, and inhabitants of the same planet, are to aid, support and protect each other. On this principle, Masonry unites men of every country, sect and opinion, and conciliates true friendship among those who might otherwise have remained at a perpetual distance.

"*Relief.*—To relieve the distressed, is a duty incumbent on all men, but particularly on Masons who profess to be linked together by indissoluble chain of sincere affection. To soothe the unhappy, to sympathize with their misfortunes to compassionate their miseries, and to restore peace to their troubled minds, is the grand aim we have in view. On this basis we form our friendships and establish our connections.

"*Truth.*—Truth is a divine attribute and the foundation of every virtue. To be good and true, is the first lesson we are taught in Masonry. On this theme we contemplate, and by its dictates endeavor, to regulate our conduct. Hence, while influencd by this principle, hypocrisy and deceit are unknown among us, sincerity and plain dealing distinguish us, and the heart and tongue join in promoting each other's welfare, and rejoicing in each other's prosperity.

"My brother, you will hereafter make yourself known among Masons by certain signs, a token, a word, and the *points of your entrance*. The signs, token and word have already been explained to you. The points of your entrance are four, namely: the *gutteral, pectoral, manual* and *pedal*—and allude to the four cardinal virtues—Temperance, Fortitude, Prudence and Justice.*

CARDINAL VIRTUES.

TEMPERANCE

"Temperance is that due restraint upon our affections and passions, which renders the body tame and governable, and frees the mind from all the allurements of vice. This virtue should be the constant practice of every Mason; as he is hereby taught to avoid excess, or the contracting of any licentious or vicious habits, the indulgence in which might lead him to disclose some of those valuable secrets which he has promised to conceal, and never reveal, and which would consequently subject him to the contempt and

---

*App. note F., page 267.

detestation of all good Masons, if not to the penalty of your obligation, which alludes to the *gutteral*.*

FORTITUDE.

"Fortitude is that noble and steady purpose of the mind, whereby we are enabled to undergo any pain, peril or danger, when prudentially deemed expedient. This virtue is equally distant from rashness and cowardice, and like the former should be deeply impressed upon the mind of every Mason, as a safeguard or security against any illegal attack that may be made by force or otherwise, to extort from him any of those valuable secrets with which he has been so solemnly entrusted, and which was emblematically represented upon your first admission into the Lodge, when you were received on the point of a sharp instrument, pressing your naked left breast, which alludes to the *pectoral*.

PRUDENCE.

"Prudence teaches us to regulate our lives and actions agreeably to the dictates of reason, and is that habit on all things relative to our present as well as to our future happiness. This virtue should be the peculiar characteristic of every Mason, not only for the government of his conduct while in the Lodge, but also when abroad in the world. It should be particularly attended to in all strange and mixed companies, never to let fall the least sign, token or word, whereby the secrets of Masonry may be unlawfully obtained, ever remembering the solemn obligation you took while kneeling on your naked left knee, your right

---

*App. note G., page 267.

forming a square, your left hand supporting the Holy
Bible, Square and Compass, your right resting thereon,
which alludes to the *manual*.

JUSTICE.

"Justice is that standard, or boundary of right,
which enables us to render unto every man his just
due, without distinction. This virtue is not only con-
sistent with divine and human laws, but is the very
cement and support of civil society; and as justice in
a great measure constitutes the really good man, so
should it be the invariable practice of every Mason
never to deviate from the minutest principles thereof,
ever remembering that solemn charge you received
while standing in the North-East corner of the Lodge,
your feet forming the angle of a square, which alludes
to the *pedal*.

"My brother, it is hoped and expected that you
will apply yourself to the study of Masonry as Entered
Apprentices served *their* masters in ancient times,
which was with freedom, fervency and zeal, emblematically represented by *chalk, charcoal* and *clay*, because there is nothing more free than *chalk*, the least
touch of which leaves a trace behind. Nothing more
fervent than *charcoal*, to which, when well ignited, the
most obdurate metals yield. Nothing more zealous
than *clay*, or Mother Earth which is constantly being
employed for man's use and is as constantly remind-
ing him, that as from it he came, so to it he must
sooner or later return.

CHARGE AT INITIATION INTO FIRST DE-
GREE.

"My Brother, having passed through the ceremonies of your initiation, I congratulate you on your
admission into our ancient and honorable Fraternity.
Ancient, as having existed from time immemorial;
honorable, as tending to make all men so, who are
strictly obedient to its precepts. It is an Institution
having for its foundation the practice of the moral
and social virtues. And to so high an eminence has
its credit been advanced, that, in every age and country, men pre-eminent for their moral and intellectual
attainments have encouraged and promoted its inter-
ests. Nor has it been thought derogatory to their dignity that monarchs have, for a season, exchanged the
sceptor for the trowel to patronize our mysteries, and
join in our assemblies.

"*As a Mason*, you are to regard the volume of the
Sacred Laws as the great light in your profession; to
consider it as the unerring standard of truth and justice, and to regulate your actions by the Divine precepts it contains. In it you will learn the important
duties you owe to God, your neighbor, and yourself.
To God, by 'never mentioning his name but with that
awe and reverence which are due from the creature
to his Creator; by imploring his aid on all your lawful
undertakings and by looking up to Him, in every
emergency, for comfort and support. *To your neighbor*, by acting with him upon the Square; by render-
ing him every kind office which justice or mercy may
require; by relieving his distresses, and soothing his
afflictions; and by doing to him, as, in similar cases,
you would that he should do unto you. And *to yourself*, by such a prudent and well-regulated course of

discipline as may best conduce to the preservation of your faculties in their fullest energy; thereby enabling you to exert the talents wherewith God has blessed you, as well to his glory as to the welfare of your fellow creatures.

"*As a Citzen,* you are enjoined to be exemplary in the discharge of your civil duties, by never proposing, or countenancing, any act which may have a tendency to subvert the peace and good order of society; by paying due obedience to the laws under whose protection you live, and by never losing sight of the allegiance due to your country.

"*As an Individual,* you are charged to practice the domestic and public virtues. Let *Temperance* chasten, *Fortitude* support, *Prudence* direct you, and *Justice* be the guide of all your actions. Be especially careful to maintain, in their fullest splendor, those true Masonic ornaments—*Brotherly Love, Relief,* and *Truth.*

"*Finally:* Be faithful to the trust committed to your care and manifest your fidelity by a strict observance of the principles of the Fraternity; and by refraining to recommend any one to a participation in our privileges, unless you have strong reasons to believe that, by a similar fidelity, he will ultimately reflect honor on our ancient Institution.*

"You will now be seated at the right of the Junior Warden in the South."

The candidate takes his seat, as directed, and the degree is ended.

The foregoing is the correct mode of conferring the first degree in Masonry; and the lecture, as here given, is precisely as it is given in the Lodge in any part of the United States.

---

*"Standard Monitor," Cook, 1903, p. 24.

CHAPTER IV.

On the night of his *initiation* the candidate, of course, knows little or nothing of the horrible and miserably degrading ceremonies through which he is passing. He is introduced in a strange and unusual manner to a strange company; and everything that happens to him from the moment he enters the Lodge-room, in a state of profound darkness, is calculated to confuse, confound and bewilder.

And immediately after the working tools are presented, the Worshipful Master (if competent to do so,) calls his attention to the most salient points in the initiatory ceremonies, and gives the *pretended* reason why each ceremony was performed, as declared in pages 80 to 84. I say here the *pretended reason,* because it is far from being the true and historic one. "Freemasonry" is but the modern name for the "Ancient Mysteries," or that secret religious worship which existed among the pagan nations of antiquity in honor of the sun-god; and every religious rite or ceremony which is now-a-days practiced in the Lodge-room, is so performed because that very same ceremony used to be practiced in the secret worship of Osiris, Baal, Bacchus, Dionysius or Tammuz in the ancient worship of the sun. In this secret worship, and in this view of the Masonic symbols and ceremonies, is contained the *real secrets* of Masonry and nowhere else; and for a full explanation of this important subject, as well as the manner in which Freemasonry or the "Mysteries" came to be revived in these modern times, the reader is further referred to the author's other work, *The Master's Carpet,* where all these rites, are examined in detail, and their origin and symbolism fully demonstrated.   But very few Masons, however, understand or care the least particle about the symbolic teachings of Masonry. The great majority of them join it for the purpose of using it in their business; and so long as they can pass themselves as Masons, and make use of the *secret language* which Masonry puts within their reach, they are perfectly satisfied and desire nothing more.

With this view, then, every Mason *must* learn the following catechism.   On the night of his initiation, the Worshipful Master introduces the candidate to some "bright" member of the Lodge, to be by him "posted" in what is technically called the "lecture." This lecture, or catechism, must be communicated and learned, orally because it is pretended to the candidate that Masonry is an *awful secret,* and that a knowledge of its profound mysteries can be acquired in no other way.   Every candidate now-a-days, however, knows better; and so, while the Lodge is bent on duping and deceiving him, he is equally bent on duping and deceiving the Lodge.   Freemasonry is a fraud and a cheat throughout; and in all its departments and degrees, satan stands behind the scenes to direct and control in every element of its existence.   Just think of a minister of the Gospel of Christ learning the following twaddle from a rumseller or an infidel after initiation!   And yet every minister must learn it, and *no stranger* can visit a Lodge, unless he can pass a satisfactory examination in all these questions and answers.   It is of the utmost importance, therefore, that they be committed well to memory.   Every candi date for the second or Fellow Craft degree must also be examined in. *open* Lodge on this ritualistic catechism; and unless he can answer correctly, and in the exact language prescribed, he cannot receive the degree.

The following is the correct method of

EXAMINATIONS.

Q. "Whence came you?"

A. "From a Lodge of the Saints John of Jerusalem."

Q. "What came you here to do?"

A. "To learn to subdue my passions, and improve myself in Masonry."

Q. "You are a Mason then, I presume?"

A. "I am, so taken and accepted among brothers and fellows."

Q. "What makes you a Mason?"

A. "My obligation."

Q. "How do you know yourself to be a Mason?"

A. "By having been often tried, never denied, and being ready to be tried again."

Q. "How shall I know you to be a Mason?"

A. "By certain signs, a token, a word, and the points of my entrance."

Q. "What are signs?"

A. "Right angles, horizontals, and perpendiculars."

Q. "Give me a sign?"

A (Makes the penal sign by drawing his right hand across the throat. See page 16.)

Q. "Has that an allusión?"

A. "It has—to the penalty of my obligation."

Should he make the due-guard, the answer would be—"It has, to the position in which my hands were placed while taking my obligation." (See page 16.)

Q. "What is a token?"

A. "A certain friendly and brotherly grip whereby one Mason may know another in the dark as well as the light."

Q. (taking candidate by the right hand as in ordinary hand shaking). "Give me a token? I hail."

A. "I conceal."

Q.   "What do you conceal?"

A. "All the secrets of Masons in Masonry, to which this token alludes."

At the word token he presses the top of his thumb hard against the first knuckle of the examiner's right hand. (See page 74).

Q. "What is this?"

A. "A grip."

Q. "Of what?"

A. "Of an Entered Apprentice Mason."

Q. "Has it a name?"

A. "It has."

Q. "Will you give it me?"

A. "I did not so receive it, neither will I so impart it."

Q. "How will you dispose of it?"

A. "I will letter and halve it with you."

Q. "Letter and begin."

A. "No, you begin."

Q. "You must begin."

A. "A."

Q. "Z."

A. "AZ."

Q. "B."

A. "O."

Q. "BO."

A. "Boaz."

Q. "Where were you made a Mason?"

A. "In a regularly constituted Lodge of Masons."

Q. "Where were you first prepared to be made a Mason?"

A. "In my heart."

Q. "Where were you secondly prepared?"

A. "In a room adjacent to a regularly constituted Lodge of Masons."

Q. "How were you prepared?"

A. "By being divested of all metals, neither naked nor clad, barefoot or shod, hoodwinked, and with a cable-tow once around my neck, in which condition I was conducted to the door of the Lodge by a friend, whom I afterward found to be a brother."

Q. "Being hoodwinked, how did you know it to be a door?"

A. "By first meeting with resistance, and afterwards gaining admission."

Q. "How gained you admission?"

A. "By three distinct knocks."

Q. "What was said to you from within?"

A. "Who comes here?"

Q. "Your answer?"

A. " 'I, James Hunt, who have long been in darkness, and now seeks to be brought to light, and to receive a part in the rights and benefits of this Worshipful Lodge, erected to God and dedicated to the Saints John, as all brothers and fellows have done before."

Q. "What were you then asked?"

A. "If it was of my own free will and accord; if I was worthy and well qualified duly and truly prepared; of lawful age and properly vouched for; all of which being answered in the affirmative, I was asked by what further rights and benefits I expected to gain admission."

Q. "Your answer?"

A. "By being a man free-born, of good report and well recommended."

Q. "How were you then disposed of?"

A. "I was directed to wait with patience until the Worshipful Master was informed of my request, and his answer returned."

Q. "What answer did he return?"

A. "'Let him enter in the name of the Lord, and be received in due form.'"

Q. "How were you received?"

A. "On the point of a sharp instrument pressing my naked left breast, which was to teach me that as that was an instrument of torture to my flesh, so should the recollection of it be to my conscience, should I ever presume to reveal the secrets of Freemasonry unlawfully."

Q. "How were you then disposed of?"

A. "I was conducted to the center of the Lodge caused to kneel and attend prayer."

Q. "After prayer, what were you asked?"

A. "In whom I put my trust."

Q. "Your answer?"

A. "'In God.'"

Q. "What followed?"

A. "I was taken by the right hand and informed that, my trust being in God, my faith was well founded; ordered to arise, follow my conductor, and fear no danger."

Q. "How were you then disposed of?"

A. "I was conducted once around the Lodge to

the Junior Warden in the South, where the same questions were asked and like answers returned as at the door."

Q. "How did the Junior Warden dispose of you?"

A. "He directed me to the Senior Warden in the West, and he to the Worshipful Master in the East, where the same questions were asked, and like answers returned, as before."

Q. "How did the Worshipful Master dispose of you?"

A. "He *ordered* me to be re-conducted to the Senior Warden in the West, who taught me how to approach the East by one upright, regular step, my feet forming the angle of a square, my body erect, at the altar before the Worshipful Master."

Q. "What did the Worshipful Master then do with you?"

A. "He made me a Mason in due form."

Q. "What is that due form?"

A. "Kneeling on my naked left knee, my right forming a square, my left hand supporting the Holy Bible, Square and Compass, my right resting thereon; in which due form, I took upon myself the solemn oath or obligation of an Entered Apprentice Mason which, is as follows:

" 'I, John Hunt, of my own free will and accord in the presence of Almighty God and this Worshipful Lodge erected to him and dedicated to the Saints John, do hereby and hereon most solemnly and sincerely promise and swear that I will always hail, ever conceal and never reveal any of the secrets, arts, parts, or points of the hidden mysteries of ancient Freemasonry, which have been heretofore, may at this time or shall at any future period be communicated to me as such to any person or persons whomsoever except it be to a true and lawful brother of this degree or within a regularly constituted Lodge of Masons, and neither unto him nor them until by strict trial due examination or legal information, I shall have found him or them as lawfully entitled to the same as I am myself. I furthermore promise and swear that I will not write, print, paint, stamp, stain, cut, carve, mark, nor engrave them, nor cause the same to be done upon anything movable or immovable, capable of receiving the least impression of a word, syllable, letter or character, whereby the same may become legible or intelligible to any person under the canopy of heaven. All this I most solmnly and sincerely promise and swear with a firm and steadfast resolution, to keep and perform the same without any equivocation, mental reservation or secret evasion of mind whatever, binding myself under a no less penalty than that of having my throat cut across, my tongue torn out by its roots and buried in the rough sands of the sea at low water mark, where the tide ebbs and flows twice in twenty-four hours, should I ever knowingly violate this my solemn obligation of an Entered Apprentice Mason. So help me God and keep me steadfast in the due performanc of the same.' "

Q. "After taking the obligation, what are you asked?"

A. "What I most desired."

Q. "Your answer?"

A. "Light."

Q. "Did you receive light?"

A. "I did, by order of the Worshipful Master and the assistance of the brethren."

Q. "Upon being brought to light what did you first discover?"

A. "The Three Great Lights in Masonry, by the assistance of the three lesser."

Q. "What are the Three Great Lights in Masonry?"

A. "The Holy Bible, Square and Compass."

Q. "What are their Masonic uses?"

A. "The Bible is given as the rule and guide of our faith, the Square, to square our actions, and the Compass to circumscribe and keep us within due bounds."

Q. "What are the three lesser lights?"

A. "Three burning tapers placed in a triangular form, representing the sun, moon, and Master of the Lodge."

Q. "Why so?"

A. "As the sun rules the day and the moon govern the night, so should the Worshipful Master endeavor to rule and govern his Lodge with equal regularity."

Q. "What did you next discover?"

A. "The Worshipful Master approaching me from the East, under the due-guard and sign of an Entered Apprentice, who, in token of friendship and brotherly love, presented me his right hand, and with it the grip and word of an Entered Apprentice Mason, *ordered* me to arise and salute the Junior and Senior Wardens as such."

Q. "After saluting the Wardens, what did you discover?"

A. "The Worshipful Master approaching me from the East a second time, who presented me with a lambskin or white leather apron, which he informed me was an emblem of innocence and the badge of a Mason, ordered be to carry it to the Senior Warden in the West who taught me how to wear it as an Entered Apprentice."

Q. "How should Entered Apprentices wear their aprons?"

A. "With the bib turned up."

Q. "After being taught how to wear your apron, how were you then disposed of?"

A. "I was reconducted to the Worshipful Master in the East, who informed me that according to an ancient custom adopted in every regular and well governed Lodge, it became necessary that I be requested to deposit something of a metalic kind, not for its intrinsic worth, but that it might be laid up amongst the records in the archives of the Lodge as a memorial, that I was there made a Mason, but upon strict search I found myself entirely destitute.

Q. "How were you then disposed of?"

A. "I was placed in the North-East corner, my feet forming the angle of a square, my body erect at the right hand of the Worshipful Master on the East. who was pleased to say that I there stood a just and upright Mason and gave it to me strictly in charge ever to walk and act as such."

Q. "With what were you then presented?"

A. "The working tools of an Entered Apprentice and taught their uses."

Q. "What are the working tools of an Entered Apprentice?"

A. "The twenty-four-inch gauge and common gavel."

Q. "What are their Masonic uses?"

A. "The twenty-four-inch gauge is an instrument made use of by operative Masons to measure and lay out their work, but we as Free and Accepted Masons are taught to make use of it for the more noble and glorious purpose of dividing our time. It being divided into twenty-four equal parts is emblematical of the twenty-four hours of the day which we are taught to divide into three equal parts, whereby we find eight hours for the service of God and a distressed worthy brother, eight for our usual vocations and eight for refreshment and sleep.

"The common gavel is an instrument made use of by operative Masons to break off the rough and super-fluous parts of stones, the better to fit them for the builder's use; but we as Free and Accepted Masons are taught to make use of it for the more noble and glorious purpose of divesting our hearts and consciences of the vices and superfluities of life, thereby fitting our minds as living stones for that spiritual building, that house not made with hands, eternal in he heavens."*

Q. "How were you then disposed of?"

A. "I was reconducted to the place where I came, invested with what I had been divested of and returned to the Lodge for further instruction."

CHAPTER V.

The second degree of Masonry is divided into two sections, the second of which is based upon the pretended tradition that at the building of King Solomon's temple 80,000 Fellow Craft workmen repaired on the sixth hour of the sixth day of the week to the middle chamber, there to receive their wages. This chamber was reached by a flight of winding stairs, as we read in 1 Kings vi. 8: "The door for the middle chamber was in the right side of the house, and they went up with *winding stairs* into the middle chamber." But to suppose that 80,000 men went up those winding stairs once a week to be paid in *corn, wine* and *oil,* is as erroneous as every other part of Freeamsonry, and that entire system is without any doubt the grandest humbug the world ever saw. Where did the 80,000 Fellow Crafts go to be paid before the middle chamber was built? Where were the supposed Junior and Senior Grand Wardens stationed before the *outer* and *inner* doors of the middle chamber were hung in their places? Brother Masons, why don't you inquire into the nature of these pretended traditions imposed upon you for pure truth, and judge for yourselves whether you ought to support such a monstrous system of error, falsehood and fraud? The reader is referred to the following pages for the Fellow Craft degree in full.

For the ceremony of opening a Lodge of Fellow Crafts "in due and ancient form," see page 7, but as the Lodge in the preceding chapter is opened on the first degree, in order to proceed with the work in regular Lodge form, it is necessary to "raise" it to the second degree which is done as follows:

The Lodge is supposed to be opened on the first degree.

Worshipful Master (one rap): "Brother Senior Warden, are you satisfied that all present are Fellow Crafts?"

Senior Warden (rising): "All present are not Fellow Crafts, Worshipful."

Worshipful Masters "All those below the degree of Fellow Craft will please retire."

The Entered Apprentices present having made the usual salute at the altar—the due-guard and sign—retire to the ante-room and generally at this stage leave the building.

Senior Warden (reports): "All present are Fellow Crafts, Worshipful."

Worshipful Master: "Brother Senior Warden, it is my order that we now dispense with labor on the first degree and resume on the second for the purpose of work; this you will communicate to the Junior Warden in the South and he to the brethren present, that all having due notice thereof may govern themselves accordingly."

Senior Warden (one rap): "Brother Junior Warden, it is the order of the Worshipful Master that we now dispense with labor on the first degree and resume on the second for work. This you will communicate to the brethren present for their government."

Junior Warden (three raps): "Brethren, it is the order of the Worshipful Master communicated to me by way of the West, that we now dispense with labor on the first degree and resume on the second for *work;* take due notice thereof and govern yourselves accordingly."

Worshipful Master: "Together, brethren."

All the brethren in unison and looking to the East make the due-guard and sign of a Fellow Craft. (See fig. pp. 26-7.) Worshipful Master gives two raps, the Senior Warden gives two, and the Junior Warden two.

Worshipful Master: "Accordingly I declare Keystone Lodge, No. 639, duly at labor on the second degree of Masonry. Brother Junior Deacon, inform the tyler. Brother Senior Deacon, arrange the lights."

The Senior Deacon elevates one point of the compass above the square, and the Junior Deacon informs the tyler as in first degree. (See page 28.) The Worshipful Master gives one rap and the brethren are seated.

Worshipful Master (one rap): "Brother Junior Deacon, you will ascertain if there are any candidates in waiting."

The Junior Deacon taking his rod steps to the altar and facing the Worshipful Master makes the due-guard and sign of a Fellow Craft. (See fig. pp. 26-7.) He then proceeds to the ante-room and finding in waiting there Brother Hunt, who has already been initiated, and being balloted for the second degree and examined in open lodge, as in page 99, he re-enters the Lodge-room, approaches the altar, makes the due-guard and sign as at retiring, and reports, as follows:

Junior Deacon: "Worshipful Master, James Hunt, an Entered Apprentice is in waiting and desires to be passed to the degree of Fellow Craft."

Worshipful Master (rising, gives one rap) "Brother Junior Deacon, you will take with you the Stewards, retire, prepare and present the candidate for the second degree. Brother Senior Deacon, you

will attend all alarms, and take charge of the door."
(One rap.)

Senior Deacon: Three raps.

Tyler: Three raps.

Exit, Junior Deacon and Stewards.

*PREPARATION.

IST SECTION.

Brother Hunt is ushered into the preparation-
room and having handed over the usual fee (often as
high as $25) to the Secretary who retires into the
Lodge, he is then *duly* and *truly* prepared for the

Dress of Candidate
Fellow Craft.

* For the meaning and origin of this ceremony of Preparation
see "Master's Carpet." pp. 251-240.

Fellow Craft degree as follows: The candidate takes off his coat, pants, vest, neck-tie, cravat, boots, stockings, in fact everything but his shirt. He then puts on an old and very often dirty pair of drawers. The *right* leg of the drawers is rolled up above the knee, the *right* breast of the shirt is turned back or folded in so as to expose the entire right breast; the right sleeve of the shirt is tucked up, exposing his right arm; a cable-tow (that is a blue rope) is passed twice around his naked arm above the elbow, a slipper with the heel slipshod is put on the left foot and a hoodwink is carefully fastened over both eyes, a white apron is then tied on with the bib turned up as an Entered Apprentice, and in this condition he is "duly and truly prepared" to be made a Fellow Craft. The Junior Deacon now leads him to the Lodge-room door, upon which he gives three loud and distinct knocks. Should the Lodge be "at ease" (that is, have recess) the Master by one rap calls the brethern to order and the Senior Deacon reports as follows:

Senior Deacon: "Worshipful Master, there is an alarm at the door of the preparation room."

Worshipful Master: "Brother Senior Deacon, attend to the alarm and report the cause."

The Senior Deacon as in the first degrees steps to the door upon which *he* also gives three loud and distinct knocks, opens the door and enquires. "Who comes here?"

Junior Deacon: "Brother James Hunt, who has been regularly initiated as an Entered Apprentice, and now seeks more light in Masonry by being passed to the degree of a Fellow Craft."

Senior Deacon: "Brother Hunt, is this of your own free-will and accord?"

Candidate: "It is."

Senior Deacon: "Brother Junior Deacon, is the candidate worthy and well qualified?"

Junior Deacon: "He is."

Senior Deacon: "Is he duly and truly prepared?"

Junior Deacon: "He is."

Senior Deacon: "Has he made a suitable proficiency in the preceding degree?"

Junior Deacon: "He has."

Senior Deacon: "Who vouches for this?"

Junior Deacon: "A brother."

Senior Deacon: "By what further right or benefit does he expect to gain admission?"

Junior Deacon: "By the benefit of a pass."

Senior Deacon: "Has he the *pass?*"

Junior Deacon: "He has it not, but I have it for him."

Senior Deacon: "Give me the pass."

The Junior Deacon steps forward a few paces and whispers in the Senior Deacon's ear the word *Shibboleth.*

Senior Deacon: "The pass is right. You will wait with patience until the Worshipful Master is informed of your request and his answer returned."

The Senior Deacon closes the door, repairs to the altar, knocks three times on the floor with his rod, makes the due-guard of a Fellow Craft (see fig. page 26) and reports as follows:

Senior Deacon: "Worshipful Master, the alarm was caused by Brother James Hunt, who has been regularly initiated as an Entered Apprentice and now seeks *more light* in Masonry by being passed to the degree of a Fellow Craft."

Worshipful Master: "Brother Senior Deacon, is this of his own free will and accord?"

Senior Deacon: "It is."

Worshipful Master: "Is the candidate worthy and well qualified?"

Senior Deacon: "He is."

Worshipful Master: "Is he duly and truly prepared?"

Senior Deacon: "He is."

Worshipful Master: "Has he made a suitable proficiency in the preceding degree?"

Senior Warden: "He has."

Worshipful Master: "Who vouches for this?"

Senior Deacon: "A brother."

Worshipful Master: "By what further right or benefit does he expect to gain admission?"

Senior Deacon: "By the benefit of a pass."

Worshipful Master: "Has he the pass?"

Senior Deacon: "He has it not, but I have it for him."

Worshipful Master: "Give me the pass."

Senior Deacon (making again the due-guard of Fellow Craft): *"Shibboleth."*

Worshipful Master: "The pass is right; since he comes endowed with all these necessary qualifications, it is my order that he enter this Lodge in the name of the Lord and be received in due form."

The Senior Deacon taking the square from off the altar, unless there be another provided, proceeds to the door which he opens wide up and says:

Senior Deacon: "It is the order of the Worshipful Master that the candidate enter this Lodge in the name of the Lord and be received in due form."

EAST.

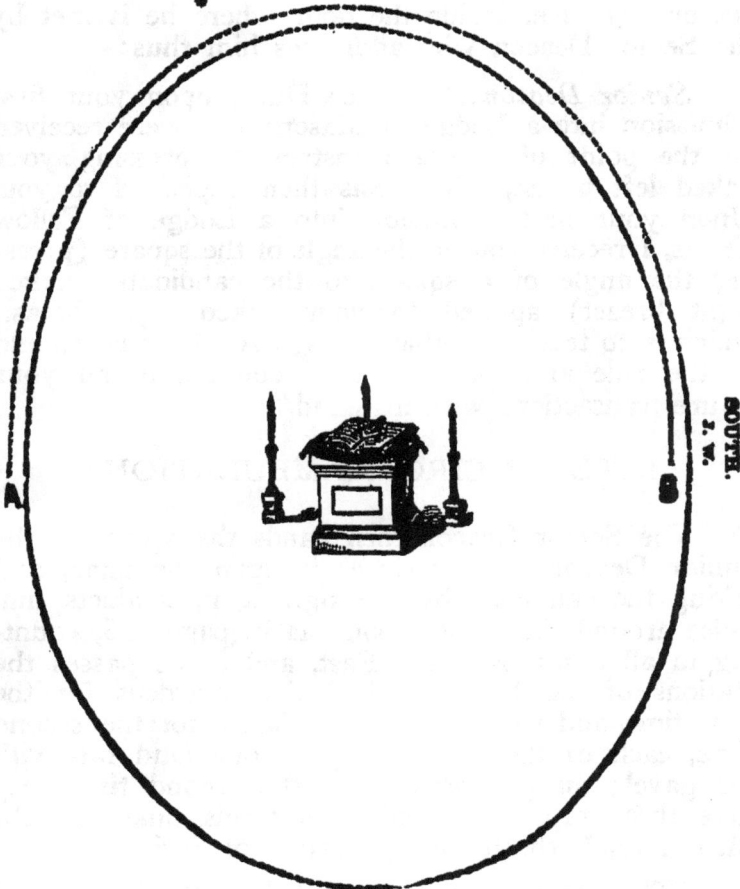

RITE OF CIRCUMAMBULATION.

*RITE OF INDUCTION.

The candidate is led in by the Junior Deacon followed by the Stewards, if any, and conducted to about six or eight feet inside the door where he is met by the Senior Deacon who addresses him thus:

Senior Deacon: "Brother Hunt, upon your first admission into a Lodge of Masons you were received on the point of a sharp instrument pressing your naked left breast, which was then explained to you. Upon your first admission into a Lodge of Fellow Crafts, I receive you on the angle of the square (pressing the angle of a square to the candidate's naked right breast) applied to your naked right breast, which is to teach you that the square of virtue should be the rule and guide of your conduct in all your future transactions with mankind."

RITE OF CIRCUMAMBULATION.

The Senior Deacon then hands the square to the Junior Deacon, who replaces it upon the altar, and taking the candidate by the right arm, conducts him twice around the Lodge-room, as in page 115, counting in all cases from the East, and as he passes the stations of the Junior and Senior Wardens for the first time and the Worshipful Master for the second time, each of these officers gives one loud rap with his gavel; on passing around the second time they give three raps each, and during this time also the Master reads the following portion of Scripture:

"Thus he showed me: and behold the Lord stood upon a wall made by a plumb line with a plumb line in his hand. And the Lord said unto me, Amos, what

---

*The present scripture reading is 1st Cor., 1 to 13 inclusive.

seest thou? And I said, a plumb line. Then said the Lord, Behold, I will set a plumb line in the midst of my people Israel. I will not pass by them any more." Amos vii. 7, 8 *

The reading of this passage is so timed as to conclude just as the candidate teaches the Junior Warden's station the second time. Having arrived in front of the Junior Warden, the Senior Deacon gives two raps on the floor with the end of his rod which is answered by one from the Junior Warden who rises to his feet and says:

Junior Warden (one rap): "Who comes here?"

Senior Deacon: "Brother James Hunt, who has been regularly initiated as an Entered Apprentice, and now seeks more light in Masonry by being passed to the degree of Fellow Craft."

Junior Warden (facing the candidate): "Brother Hunt, is this of your own free-will and accord?"

Candidate: "It is."

Junior Warden: "Brother Senior Deacon, is the candidate worthy and well qualified?"

Senior Deacon: "He is."

Junior Warden: "Is he duly and truly prepared?"

Senior Deacon: "He is."

Junior Warden: "Has he made a suitable proficiency in the preceding degree?".

Senior Deacon: "He has."

Junior Warden: "Who vouches for this?"

Senior Deacon: "A brother."

Junior Warden: "By what further right or benefit does he expect to gain this favor?"

Senior Deacon: "By the benefit of a pass."

---

* "Standard Monitor," Cook, 1903, p. 29.
* For the meaning and origin of this ceremony, see "Master's Carpet." pp. 268-272.

Junior Warden: "Has he the pass?"

Senior Deacon: "He has it not, but I have it for him."

Junior Warden: "Give me the pass."

The Senior Deacon approaches closer to the Junior Warden, and whispers in his ear the word *Shibboleth.*

Junior Warden: "The pass is right. You will conduct the candidate to the Senior Warden in the West for further examination."

The Senior Deacon with candidate then approaches the Senior Warden's station and gives three raps with his rod as before.

Senior Warden (1 rap): "Who comes here?"

Senior Deacon: "Brother Hunt, who has been regularly initiated as an Entered Apprentice and now seeks *more light* in Masonry by being passed to the degree of a Fellow Craft."

Senior Warden (turning to candidate): "Brother Hunt, is this of your own free will and accord?"

Candidate: "It is."

Senior Warden: "Brother Senior Deacon, is the candidate worthy and well qualified?"

Senior Deacon: "He is," etc., etc.

Precisely the same dialogue takes place here as at the Junior Warden's station, which see above, and at the conclusion of which the Senior Warden says:

Senior Warden: "The pass is right. You will conduct the candidate to the Worshipful Master in the East for further examination."

The candidate is now conducted towards the East and placed in front of the Master's chair, who in response to the Senior Deacon's raps, enquires in a deep tone of voice:

Worshipful Master: "Who comes here?"

Senior Deacon: "Brother James Hunt, who has been regularly initiated as an Entered Apprentice and now seeks more light in Masonry by being *passed* to the degree of Fellow Craft."

Worshipful Master (turning to candidate): "Brother Hunt, is this of your own free will and accord?"

Candidate: "It is."

Worshipful Master: "Brother Senior Deacon, is the candidate worthy and well qualified?"

Senior Deacon: "He is."

Worshipful Master: "Is he duly and truly prepared?"

Senior Deacon: "He is."

Worshipful Master: "Has he made a suitable proficiency in the preceding degree?"

Senior Deacon: "He has."

Worshipful Master: "Who vouches for this?"

Senior Deacon: "A brother."

Worshipful Master: "By what further right or benefit does he expect to obtain this favor?"

Senior Deacon: "By the benefit of a pass."

Worshipful Master (in some astonishment): "Has *he the pass?*"

Senior Deacon: "He has it not, but I have it for him."

Worshipful Master: "Give me the pass."

The Senior Deacon approaches close to Master's chair and whispers into his ear the word *Shibboleth.*

Worshipful Master: "The pass is right, since he comes endowed with all these necessary qualifications it is my *order* that you re-conduct him to the Senior Warden in the West who will teach him to approach the East by two upright regular steps, his feet forming the angle of a square, his body erect at the altar before the Worshipful Master."

The Senior Deacon re-conducts the candidate to the Senior Warden whose attention he attracts by simply giving one rap with his rod on the floor.

Senior Deacon: "Brother Senior Warden, it is the order of the Worshipful Master that you teach the candidate to approach the East by two upright regular steps, his feet forming the angle of a square, his body erect at the altar before the Worshipful Master."

Senior Warden: "Brother Senior Deacon, you will face the candidate towards the East."

The Senior Deacon taking the candidate by the arm wheels him around so as to have him face the Worshipful Master. The Senior Warden then leaves his seat and approaching the candidate, says:

Senior Warden: "Brother Hunt, you will take the Entered Apprentice step (stepping off one step with left foot and bringing the heel of the right to the hollow of the left, see page 68). You will now step off one step with your right foot bringing the heel of the left to the hollow of the right, forming the angle of a square." (Should the candidate not be able to do this, or do it awkwardly, the Senior Warden instructs him.) "Stand erect."

The Senior Warden then returning to his station and making the due-guard of a Fellow Craft, exclaims:

Senior Warden: "In order, Worshipful."

*RITE OF SECRECY.

Worshipful Master (rising from his seat, gives 3 raps): "Brother Hunt, you are now standing at the altar of Masonry for the second time, but before proceeding further, it becomes my duty as the Worshipful Master of this Lodge to inform you that it will be necessary that you take upon yourself a solemn oath or obligation pertaining to this degree, and I can assure you upon the honor of a man and a Mason that in this obligation there is nothing that will conflict with any duty you owe to God, your country, your family, your neighbor or yourself. In your advancement thus far you have repeatedly assured us it was of your own free will and accord; if you are still of the same mind, you will advance to our altar."

The Senior Deacon now leads the candidate towards the altar.

"Kneel on your naked right knee, your left forming a square, your right hand resting on the Holy Bible, square and compass, your left arm forming a right angle supported by a square." (The Senior Deacon of course places him correctly in each of these positions.) In some Lodges the candidate, in raising his left arm so that the angle of a square is formed at the elbow, is made to take hold of the Senior Deacon's rod placed perpendicular, while in others his left

* For the meaning and origin of this ceremony, see "Master's Carpet," pp. 273-280.

arm is supported by a square held in place by the
Senior Deacon. The Worshipful Master now gives
three raps which is a signal for all the brethren except
the Senior Warden to arrange themselves in two ranks
on either side of the altar, the Master removing his
hat, approaches the kneeling candidate and continues:

Worshipful Master: "In which due form you
will say 'I,' repeat your name in full and say after me:

OBLIGATION.

"I, James Hunt, of my own free will and accord,
in the presence of Almighty God and this Worshipful
Lodge erected to him and dedicated to the Saints John,
do hereby and hereon (here the Master places his right
hand on that of the candidate) most solemnly and
sincerely promise and swear that I will always hail,
ever conceal and never reveal any of the secret arts,
parts or points of the Fellow Craft degree, to any person or persons whomsoever, except it be to a true and
lawful brother of this degree, or within a regularly
constituted Lodge of Fellow Crafts; and neither unto
him nor them until by strict trial, due examination, or
legal information I shall have found him or them as
lawfully entitled to the same as I am myself.

I furthermore promise and swear that I will
conform to and abide by all the laws, rules and regulations of the Fellow Craft degree so far as the same
shall come to my knowledge.

"Furthermore, that I will answer and obey all
due signs and summons sent to me from a lodge of
Fellow Crafts or given to me by a brother of this degree if within the length of my cable-tow.

"Furthermore, that I will aid and assist all worthy
distressed brother Fellow Crafts, I knowing them to

be such, so far as my ability will permit without material injury to myself.

"Furthermore, that I will not cheat, wrong nor defraud a lodge of Fellow Crafts, nor a brother of this degree, nor supplant him in any of his laudable undertakings.

"All this I most solemly and sincerely promise and swear with a firm and steadfast resolution to keep and perform the same, without any equivocation, mental reservation or secret evasion of mind whatever, binding myself under a no less penalty than that of having my left breast torn open (see sign of Fellow Craft, page 27), my heart plucked out and given as a prey to the beasts of the field and the fowls of the air should I ever knowingly violate this my solemn obligation of a Fellow Craft Mason, so help me God and keep me steadfast in the due performance of the same."

Worshipful Master: "In token of your sincerity, you will detach your hands and kiss the Bible." (Candidate removes his hands and kisses the book.)

Worshipful Master (resuming his hat): "Brother Senior Deacon, you will release the brother from the cable-tow he is bound to us by an obligation, a tie stronger than human hands can impose."

Senior Deacon removes the rope from off the candidate's right arm.

Worshipful Master (stepping back eight or ten paces): "Bro. Hunt, in your present condition what do you most desire?"

Candidate (prompted by Senior Deacon): "More light in Masonry."

Worshipful Master: "Bro. Senior Deacon and brethren, you will assist me in bringing this brother from darkness to light."

The two Stewards now raise their rods bringing their points together over the Master's head, thus forming a kind of triangular arch. (See Entered Apprentice degree, page 71.)

RITE OF ILLUMINATION.

Worshipful Master: "In the beginning God created the heavens and the earth. And the earth was without form and void, and darkness was upon the face of the deep and the Spirit of God moved upon the face of the waters and God said, 'Let there be light, and there was light.' In humble commemoration of which august event we Masonically say, 'Let there be light.' "

The Master and all the brethren together make the due-guard of a Fellow Craft, retaining their hands in the position for a few seconds, at the same time as quick as the Master utters the word "light" the Senior Deacon standing behind the candidate snatches off the hoodwink, the entire scene being intended to make a deep impression on his mind and give him an exalted idea of the beauty and grandeur of Masonic light. The Master and brethren then drop their hands and the Worshipful Master continues:

Worshipful Master: "And there is light."*

Worshipful Master: "Upon being brought to light in this degree, you discover the three great lights in Masonry as before, with this difference, one point of the compass is elevated above the square which is to teach you that you have as yet received light in Masonry but partially."

The Worshipful Master again steps back a few

---

*For the meaning and origin of this rite, see "Master's Carpet," pp. 281-286.

paces and the Stewards crossing their rods as before, the Senior Deacon addressing the candidate, says:

Senior Deacon: "Brother Hunt, you now behold the Worshipful Master approaching you from the East (Master steps off one step with the right foot, bringing the heel of the left to the hollow of the right) under the due-guard (makes the due-guard, see fig. page 26) and sign (makes the sign, see fig. page 27) of a Fellow Craft Mason."

Worshipful Master (to candidate): "An Entered Apprentice steps off with his left foot, bringing the heel of the right to the hollow of the left, forming the angle of a square and this is the first step in Masonry. A Fellow Craft steps off with his right foot bringing the heel of the left to the hollow of the right forming also the angle of a square, and this is the second step in Masonry. This was given you as the due-guard, and this as the sign of an Entered Apprentice, which were then explained to you. This is the due-guard of a Fellow Craft and alludes to the position in which your hands were placed, while taking your obligation. This is the sign of a Fellow Craft and alludes to the penalty of your obligation. In token of the continuance of friendship and brotherly love, I present you my right hand and with it the pass, token of the pass, grip and word of a Fellow Craft, but as you are uninstructed, I will explain them with Brother Senior Deacon. Take me as I take you.

*RITE OF INTRUSTING.

The Master takes the candidate by the right hand as in ordinary hand-shaking, pressing the top of his thumb hard against the first knuckle joint of the first finger. (See fig. page 74.)

Worshipful Master: "Will you be off or from?" (turning to Senior Deacon).

Senior Deacon (standing near the candidate): rom."

Worshipful Master: "From what to what?"

Senior Deacon: "From the grip of an Entered pprentice to the pass-grip of a Fellow Craft."

Worshipful Master: "Pass. What is this?"

Senior Deacon moves the candidate's thumb from the first knuckle of the Master's hand to the space between the first and second knuckles, the Master at the same time moving his thumb to the same space of the candidate's right hand. (See page 140.)

Senior Deacon: "The pass-grip of a Fellow Craft."

Worshipful Master: "Has it a name?"

Senior Deacon: "It has."

Worshipful Master: "Will you give it to me?"

Senior Deacon: "I did not so receive it neither will I so impart it."

Worshipful Master: "How will you dispose of it?"

Senior Deacon: "I will syllable it with you?"

Worshipful Master: "Syllable and begin."

Senior Deacon: "No, you begin."

Worshipful Master: "You must begin."

Senior Deacon: "Bo."

Worshipful Master: "Shib."

Senior Deacon: "Leth."

Worshipful Master: "Shibbo."

Senior Deacon (pronouncing): "Shibboleth."

Worshipful Master (turning to Senior Deacon): "The pass is right. Will you be off or from?"

Senior Deacon: "From."

Worshipful Master: "From what to what?"

Senior Deacon: "From the pass-grip of a Fellow Craft to the real grip of the same."

Worshipful Master: "Pass. What is this?"

Senior Deacon removes the candidate's thumb to the second knuckle of the Master's right hand, while the Master removes his thumb to the second knuckle of the candidate's hand. (See page 142.)

Senior Deacon: "The real grip of a Fellow Craft."

Worshipful Master: "Has it a name?"

Senior Deacon: "It has."

Worshipful Master: "Will you give it to me?"

Senior Deacon: "I did not so receive it neither will I so impart it."

Worshipful Master: "How will you dispose of it?"

Senior Deacon: "I will letter it with you."

Worshipful Master: "Letter and begin."

Senior Deacon: "No, you begin."

Worshipful Master: "You must begin."

Senior Deacon: "A."

Worshipful Master: "J."

Senior Deacon: "C."
Worshipful Master: "H."
Senior Deacon: "I."
Worshipful Master: "N."
Senior Deacon: "Ja."
Worshipful Master: "Chin."
Senior Deacon (pronouncing): "Jachin."
Worshipful Master: "The grip is right, the word is right. You will arise and salute the Junior and Senior Wardens as a Fellow Craft."

Worshipful Master (one rap): "How is it in the South, Brother Junior Warden?"

Junior Warden (rising and making the due-guard): "All right in the South, Worshipful."

Worshipful Master (one rap) (to Senior Deacon): "How is it in the West, Brother Senior Warden?"

Senior Warden (rising and making due-guard): "All right in the West, Worshipful."

Worshipful Master (one rap) (to Senior Deacon): "Brother Senior Deacon, you will re-conduct the brother to the Senior Warden in the West who will teach him how to wear his apron as a Fellow Craft."

The candidate here should not be led around the altar, but simply re-conducted to the Senior Warden's station where the Senior Deacon gives one rap on the floor with the end of his rod, as usual, which brings the Senior Warden to his feet and the Senior Deacon says:

Senior Deacon: "Brother Senior Warden, it. is the order of the Worshipful Master that you teach the brother how to wear his apron as a Fellow Craft."

*RITE OF INVESTITURE.

Senior Warden: "My brother, Masonic tradition informs us that at the building of King Solomon's Temple, Fellow Crafts wore their aprons with the bib turned down and the left corner turned up in the form of a triangle to serve as a receptacle for their working tools. As a speculative Fellow Craft you will therefore wear yours in the manner that the three sides of the triangle thus formed may symbolize the fidelity, understanding and skill, which should characterize your work as a Fellow Craft." And candidate is re-conducted to the East.

WORKING TOOLS.

The Master here produces a set of miniature tools made of wood and sometimes very richly ornamented, especially if the Lodge is a silk stocking or aristocratic one. In poorer lodges they are compelled to be satisfied with poorer and less costly implements.

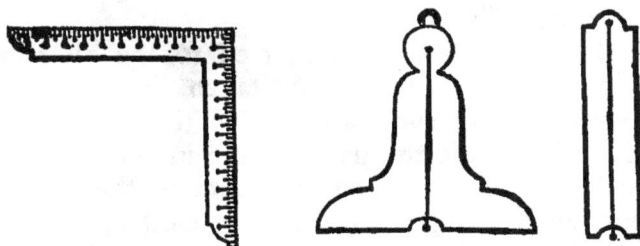

Worshipful Master: "As you are now clothed as a Fellow Craft you are entitled to your working tools. The working tools of a Fellow Craft are the plumb, square and level.

Worshipful Master: "The *plumb* is an instrument made use of by operative Masons to try perpendiculars, the *square* to square their work and the *level* to prove horizontals (hands the working tools to candidate), but we as free and accepted Masons are taught to make use of them for more noble and glorious purposes. The plumb admonishes us to walk uprightly in our several stations before God and man, squaring our actions by the *square* of virtue, ever remembering that we are traveling upon the *level* of time to that undiscovered country from whose bourne no traveler returns* (Receives the working tools from candidate.) You will now be re-conducted to the place from whence you came, invested with what you have been divested of, and in accordance with an ancient custom adopted in every regular and well-governed Lodge, it will be necessary that you make a regular advance through a *porch* by a flight of *winding stairs* consisting of three, five and seven steps, to a place representing the *middle chamber* of King Solomon's Temple, where you will find the Worshipful Master, who will give you instructions relative to the wages and jewels of a Fellow Craft."

The candidate is conducted to the altar by the Senior Deacon where he is taken in charge by the Stewards, or in their absence by the Junior Deacon, and having made the usual salute in this degree, dueguard and sign, they conduct him to the preparation room where he gets on his own clothing as speedily as possible. This ends the first section of the degree.

While the candidate is dressing the Lodge is usually called from *labor* to *refreshment,* or in common, everyday language the members have a short recess: This is announced by the Master saying, "The Lodge will be at ease until the sound of the gavel in the

---

* "Standard Monitor," Cook, 1903, p. 30.

East," or "The Lodge will be called from labor to refreshment until the sound of the gavel in the East." During this short recess the Lodge is prepared for the second section of the degree or as Masons technically term it, "the middle chamber work," which is done as follows:

In every well-furnished Lodge there are two large pillars, from eight to ten and sometimes fifteen feet high, permanently fixed inside the "preparation-room" door, one on each side, and about five or six feet from it. These pillars represent the two celebrated pillars, Boaz and Jachin, at the *entrance* of the *porch* of King Solomon's temple and of which mention is made in 1 Kings vi. 8. They are only brought into requisition in the second section of this degree.

Some brother, generally the Senior Deacon, brings out three pieces of oil-cloth or large painting on easel which he lays on the floor about five feet apart and so arranged as to very faintly represent a flight of winding stairs.

On the first piece is painted the representation of three steps and the letters E. A., F. C., M. M., that is Entered Apprentice, Fellow Craft, and Master Mason; also the letters W. M., S. W., J. W., denoting Worshipful Master, Senior Warden, and Junior Warden.

On the second piece of canvass is a representation of five steps, also five pillars or columns to denote the five orders of architecture and the letters H. S. F. S. and T., to signify the five human senses—Hearing, Seeing, Feeling, Smelling and Tasting, whose initials these letters are.

On the third piece are represented seven steps and the letters G. R. L. A. G. M. A., the initials of Grammar, Rhetoric, Logic, Arithmetic, Geometry, Music and Astronomy, comprising the so-called seven liberal arts and sciences, a knowledge of which Freemasonry among its numerous other bombastic claims professes to impart to its hoodwinked members.

Everything in the Lodge being thus properly arranged, and the candidate having finished his toilet, the Master calls the Lodge to order and the Senior Deacon taking his rod places the candidate immediately inside the door of the preparation-room between the pillars, Boaz and Jachin, and commences the second section or "middle chamber work" of the Fellow Craft degree, as follows :*

SECOND SECTION.

Senior Deacon (standing by the side of candidate inside the door) : "My brother, Masonry is considered under two denominations—Operative and Speculative.

"By Operative Masonry we allude to a proper application of the useful rules of architecture whence a structure will derive figure, strength and beauty, and whence will result a due proportion and a just correspondence in all its parts. It furnishes us with dwellings and convenient shelter from the vicissitudes and inclemencies of the seasons, and while it displays the effects of human wisdom as well in the choice as in the arrangement of the sundry materials of which an edifice is composed, it demonstrates that a fund of science and industry is implanted in man for the best, most salutary and beneficent purposes.

"By Speculative Masonry we learn to subdue the passions, act upon the square, keep a tongue of good report, maintain secrecy, and practice charity. It is so far interwoven with religion as to lay us under obligations to pay that rational homage to the Deity which at once constitutes our duty and our happiness. It leads the contemplative to view with reverence and admiration the glorious works of creation and inspires him with the most exalted ideas of the perfections of his Divine Creator.*

"Our ancient brethren wrought in operative and speculative, but we work in speculative only. They wrought six days before receiving their wages, but did not work on the seventh, because 'In six days God created the heavens and the earth and rested upon the seventh day.' The seventh, therefore, our ancient brethren consecrated as a day of rest from their labors, thereby enjoying more frequent opportunities to contemplate the glorious works of the creation and to adore their great Creator.*

"The first object to which I will call your attention on your passing to the 'middle chamber' is a representation of two brazen pillars (Senior Deacon points to the pillars), one on your left hand and the other on your right. The one on your left hand (pointing to it) is called Boaz and denotes *strength;* the one on the right is called Jachin and denotes *establishment.* Taken together they allude to a promise of God to David that he would establish his kingdoms in strength. They were cast on the plains of Jordan in the clay ground, between Succoth and Zaredatha (where all the brazen vessels of King Solomon's temple were cast) by one Hiram Amon, or Abi, a widow's son of the tribe of Naphtali. They were cast hollow to serve as repository for the archives of Masonry and to guard against accident by inundation or conflagration.

---

* "Standard Monitor," Cook, 1903, p. 31.
* See Monitor.
* App. note I. p. 267.

"They were thirty-five (35) cubits in height, twelve in circumference and about four (4) in diameter. They were adorned by chapiters of five (5) cubits each, making in all forty (40) cubits high.

"These chapiters were ornamented with lily-work, net work and pomegranates, denoting *peace, unity* and *plenty.* The lily-work from its purity and the retired situation in which it grows denotes peace; the network from the intimate connection of its parts denotes unity, and the promegranate from the exuberance of its seed denotes plenty.

"These pillars were further adorned by pommels on three tops, representing globes, denoting the universality of Masonry. Let us pass on.

Senior Deacon (to candidate) : "Let us pass on."

They pass out between the two pillars and proceeding a few paces arrive at the first piece of *oilcloth,* which is supposed to be the foot of the winding stairs, and stop.

Senior Deacon (to candidate) : "The next object to which I will call your attention is a representation of a flight of *winding stairs* consisting of three (3),* five (5), and seven (7) steps. The number three alludes to the three degrees which every Master Mason Lodge confers. Also to the three principal officers of the Lodge, viz.: the Worshipful Master, Senior Warden and Junior Warden."

They move on a few paces more, the candidate being made to walk over the supposed "three steps," and having arrived at the second piece of oil-cloth they again halt and the Senior Deacon proceeds:

Senior Deacon: "We next arrive at a representation of the 'five steps.' Let us pass on." The number five alludes to the five orders in architecture and the five human senses.

---

* Append'x note L. page 268.·

"By order in architecture is meant a system of all the members, proportions and ornaments of colums and pilasters, or it is a regular arrangement of the projecting parts of a building which, united with those of a column, form a beautiful, perfect and complete whole.

"From the first formation of society order in architecture may be traced. When the rigor of seasons obliged men to contrive shelter from the inclemency of the weather, we learn that they first planted trees on end and then laid others across to support a covering. The bands which connected those trees at top and bottom are said to have given rise to the idea of the base and capital of pillars, and from this simple hint originally proceeded the more improved art of architecture.*

"The five orders in architecture are thus classed: namely, the Tuscan, the Doric, the Ionic, the Corinthian and the Composite."

In some lodges, and especially in cases where the Senior Deacon is desirous of exhibiting his superior attainments in Masonic knowledge, he here gives a lengthy description of the different orders, all of which, however, he has memorized from the Monitor, and is, therefore, termed monitorial work. In country lodges this is scarcely ever done, and indeed in the best of city lodges it is never more than tiresome and meaningless to the candidate and a bore to the members generally. The following, therefore, is all that is usually repeated and indeed all that the lodge wants to listen to:

Senior Deacon (to candidate): "The ancient and original orders of architecture, however, as revered by Masons, are no more than three: the Doric, the

---
* "Standard Monitor," Cook, 1903, p. 38.

Ionic and the Corinthian, which were invented by the Greeks. To these the Romans have added two—the Tuscan which they made plainer than the Doric, and the Composite which was more ornamental, if not more beautiful than the Corinthian. The first three orders, alone, however, show invention and particular character and are essentially different from each other; the two others have nothing but what is borrowed, and differ only by accident; the Tuscan is but the Doric, in its earliest state, and the Composite is only the Corinthian enriched with the Ionic. To the Greeks, therefore, and not to the Romans, are we indebted for all that is great, judicious and distinct in architecture.*

"The human senses to which this number five has a further allusion are Hearing, Seeing, Feeling, Smelling and Tasting; the three first of which, namely, *hearing, seeing* and *feeling,* have always been considered as peculiarly essential to Masons; for by *hearing* we hear the word, *seeing* we see the sign, and *feeling* we feel the grip whereby one Mason may know another in the dark as well as in the light."
Appendix note L., p. 268.

Here, as in the case of the orders of architecture, the Senior Deacon, wishing to "show off," repeats a lot of trash, dilating on the five senses, which he learns from some Monitor (see Sickles' Ahiman Reson, pages 138-145; also Mackey and Webb).

Senior Deacon (to candidate) : "Let us pass on."

They then move on a few paces further and arrive at the third piece of oil-cloth, where the candidate is again halted by the Senior Deacon, who says:

Senior Deacon: "We next arrive at the representation of the 'seven steps.' The number seven

---

* "Standard Monitor," Cook, 1903, p. 84.

alludes to the seven liberal arts and sciences, which are Grammar, Rhetoric, Logic, Arithmetic, Geometry, Music and Astronomy."*

A Senior Deacon possessed of the spirit of egotism and vain-glory, having learned his part from Sickles, Moore or Mackey, would, especially if prominent visitors were present, rehearse here a pedantic and unintelligible essay on the beauty and usefulness of the liberal arts and sciences, while at the same time he may know no more (and indeed never does) of what he is repeating than a North American savage does of the transit of Venus; but, as the whole matter is printed and accessible to every member, the silly vanity of the Senior Deacon is very seldom tolerated, and hence he almost always contents himself with the following:

Senior Deacon: "I will, however, call your attention more particularly to the fifth science or Geometry, being that which is most highly esteemed among Masons."

GEOMETRY

"Is that science which treats of the powers and properties of magnitudes in general, where length, breadth and thickness are considered, from a *point* to a *line,* from a line to a *superficies,* and from a superficies to a *solid.*

"A *point* is a position without dimensions.

"A *line* is a figure of one capacity, namely, length.

"A *superficies* is a figure of two dimensions, length and breadth.

"A *solid* is a figure of three dimensions, namely, length, breadth and thickness.

"By this science the architect is enabled to construct his plans and execute his designs; the general, to arrange his soldiers; the engineer, to mark out grounds for encampments; the geographer, to give us the dimensions of the world, and all things therein contained; to delineate the extent of seas, and specify the divisions of empires, kingdoms and provinces. By it also, the astronomer is enabled to make his observations and to fix the duration of times and seasons, years and cycles.

"In fine, geometry is the foundation of architecture, and the root of the mathematics."*

Senior Deacon (to candidate):   "Let us pass on."

Having walked over the last strip of oil-cloth representing the "seven steps" the Senior Deacon continues:

Senior Deacon: "We next arrive at a representation of the *outer door* of the middle chamber of King Solomon's temple which we shall find strongly guarded by the Junior Warden in the South. Let us approach the place."

By this time they have arrived in front of the Junior Warden's chair where the Senior Deacon gives three raps with the end of his rod on the floor. The Junior Warden rising to his feet, says:

Junior Warden: "Who comes here?"

Senior Deacon: "A Fellow Craft on his way to the middle chamber to receive instructions relative to wages and jewels of a Fellow Craft."

Junior Warden: "How does he expect to gain admission?"

Senior Deacon: "By the pass and token of the pass."

* "Standard Monitor." Cook, 1908, p. 86.

Junior Warden: "Give me the pass."

Senior Deacon (answering for candidate): "Shibboleth."

Junior Warden: "What does it denote?"

Senior Deacon: "Plenty."

Junior Warden: "How is it represented?"

Senior Deacon: "By a sheaf of corn suspended near a waterfall."

Junior Warden: "Whence originated this word as a pass?"

Senior Deacon: "In consequence of a quarrel between Jephthah, judge of Israel, and the Ephraimites, having long been a turbulent and rebellious people whom Jephthah had sought to subdue by wise and lenient measures, but without effect. They being highly incensed and fraught with vengeance at not being called upon to fight and share in the rich spoils of the Ammonitish war, gathered together a mighty army and crossed the river Jordan to give Jephthah battle; but he being apprised of their intention assembled the men of Gilead, gave *them* battle and put them to flight; and to make his victory more complete he placed guards at the several passes on the banks of the river Jordan and commanded them, that, 'If any should attempt to pass that way, demand of them say, "Say now shibboleth,"' but they being of a different tribe could not frame to pronounce it right and said 'sibboleth,' which trifling difference proved them enemies and cost them their lives. And there fell at that time of the Ephraimites, forty and two thousand, since which time this word has been adopted as a pass whereby to gain admission into every regular and well-governed lodges of the Fellow Crafts."

Junior Warden (to Senior Deacon): "**Give me the token.**"

Senior Deacon taking Junior Warden by the right hand, presses the top of his thumb hard against the space between the first and second knuckle. (See page 126.)

The *pass grip* of a Fellow Craft, or as it is termed here, the *token* of a pass, is made as follows:

The Junior Warden takes the candidate by the right hand as in ordinary hand-shaking, and presses the top of his thumb hard against the space *between the first and second knuckle* joints of the first two

fingers; the candidate also presses his thumb on the corresponding part of the Junior Warden's hand. (See figure above.)

Junior Warden: "The pass is right, the token is right; pass on."

Senior Deacon (to candidate, moving on slowly): "We shall next arrive at a place representing the *inner door* of the middle-chamber which we shall find more strongly guarded by the Senior Warden in the West. Let us approach the place."

About this time they arrive in front of the Senior Warden's chair, where the Senior Deacon gives two raps as before, calling the Senior Warden to his feet.

Senior Warden: "Who comes here?"

Senior Deacon: "A Fellow Craft on his way to the middle chamber, to receive instructions relative to the wages and jewels of a Fellow Craft."

Senior Warden: "How does he expect to gain admission?"

Senior Deacon: "By the *grip* and *word* of a Fellow Craft."

Senior Warden: "Give me the grip."

Senior Deacon taking Senior Warden by the right hand presses the top of his thumb hard against the first knuckle of the second finger (see figure on next page).

Senior Warden: "What is this?" (pressing his thumb on the corresponding knuckle of Senior Deacon's hand).

Senior Deacon: "The real grip of a Fellow Craft."

Senior Warden: "Has it a name?"

Senior Deacon: "It has."

Senior Warden: "Will you give it to me?"

Senior Deacon: "I did not so receive it, neither will I so impart it."

Senior Warden: "How will you dispose of it?"

Senior Deacon: "I will letter it with you."

Senior Warden: "Letter and begin."

Senior Deacon: "No, you begin."

Senior Warden: "You must begin."

Senior Deacon: "A."

Senior Warden: "J."

Senior Deacon: "C."

Senior Warden: "H."

Senior Deacon: "I."

Senior Warden: "N."

Senior Deacon: "Ja."

Senior Warden: "Chin."

Senior Deacon: "Jachin."

Senior Warden: "What does it denote?"

Senior Deacon: "Establishment."

Senior Warden: "How is it represented?"

Senior Deacon: "By the right-hand pillar at the entrance of the porch of King Solomon's temple."

The *real grip* of a Fellow Craft is given in the following manner:

The Senior Warden takes the candidate by the right hand as in ordinary hand-shaking, and presses the top of his thumb hard on the second knuckle—the candidate presses his thumb against the same knuckle of the Senior Warden's hand. (See figure above.) For the manner of giving the *pass grip* and *real grip* in full, see pages 126-127.

Senior Warden: "The *grip* is right, the *word* is right; pass on."

The Senior Deacon and candidate moving slowly from the Senior Warden's chair towards the East, the Senior Deacon says:

Senior Deacon (to candidate): "You have now arrived within a representation of the middle chamber, where you will find the Worshipful Master, who will give you instructions relative to the wages and jewels of a Fellow Craft."

The candidate is by this time in front of the Master's chair, where he is left standing by the Senior Deacon who takes his usual seat.

Worshipful Master (rising and addressing candidate): "My brother, you have now arrived within a representation of the middle chamber of King Solomon's temple, where you will be received and recorded as a Fellow Craft. (Turning to Secretary) Brother Secretary, you will please make the record."

Secretary, pretending to write, answers:

Worshipful Master (to candidate): "The first object which most particularly attracted your attention on your passing hither was a representation of two brazen pillars, one on the right hand, the other on your left, which were explained to you by your conductor. After passing the pillars you arrived at a flight of winding stairs, consisting of three, five and seven steps, which were also explained to you. After passing the stairs you arrived at a representation of the outer door of the middle chamber, which you found strongly guarded by the Junior Warden in the South, who demanded of you the *pass* and *token* of the *pass* of a Fellow Craft. After passing the outer door, you arrived at the inner door of the middle chamber, which you found more strongly guarded by the Senior Warden in the West, who demanded of you the grip and word of a Fellow Craft. You next arrived within the middle chamber, where you were received and recorded as a Fellow Craft and are now entitled to an explanation of the wages and jewels of a Fellow Craft. The wages of a Fellow Craft are *corn, wine* and *oil,* emblematical of the corn of nourishment, the wine of refreshment, and the oil of joy; denoting *plenty, health* and *peace.* The jewels of a Fellow Craft are the *attentive ear,* the *instructive tongue,* and the *faithful breast.* (The attentive ear receives the sound from the instructive tongue, and the mysteries of Masonry are safely lodged in the repository of faithful breasts.")*

Worshipful Master (pointing to the letter G, suspended over the Master's chair, continues): "I will

* See Appendix note N, p. 269,

now call your attention to the letter G, which you
see above the Master's chair. It is the initial of

GEOMETRY.

"Geometry, is the basis on which the superstruc-
ture of Masonry is erected. By geometry we may
curiously trace nature through her various windings,
to her most concealed recesses. By it we discover
the power, wisdom and goodness of the Grand
Artificer of the Universe, and view with delight the
proportions which connect this vast machine. By it
we discover how the planets move in their respective
orbits, and demonstrate their various revolutions. By
it we account for the return of the seasons and the
variety of scenes which each season displays to the
discerning eye. Numberless worlds are around us, all
framed by the same Divine Artist, which roll through
the vast expanse, and are all conducted by the same
unerring law of nature.

"A survey of nature, and the observation of her
beautiful proportions, first determined man to imitate
the divine plan, and study symmetry and order. This
gave rise to societies; and birth to every useful art.
The architect began to design, and the plans which he
laid down, being improved by time and experience,
have produced works which are the wonder and admiration of every age.

"The lapse of time, the ruthless hand of ignorance,
and the devastations of war, have laid waste and destroyed many valuable monuments of antiquity, on
which the utmost exertions of human genius had been
employed. Even the temple of Solomon, so spacious
and magnificent, and constructed by so many celebrated artists, escaped not the unsparing ravages of

barbarous ɪorce. Freemasonry, notwithstanding, has still survived.

"The *attentive ear* receives the sound from the *instructive tongue,* and the mysteries of Masonry are safely lodged in the repository of *faithful breasts.* Tools and implements of architecture, symbols most expressive, selected by the fraternity, to imprint on the memory wise and serious truths; and thus, through a succession of ages, are transmitted, unimpaired, the most excellent tenets of our institution.

"But, my brother, (gives 3 raps, calls up lodge) the letter (pointing to the G) has a still higher and holier significance (gives three raps calling up the entire lodge.*) It alludes to the sacred name of Deity, before whom all, from the youngest Entered Apprentice who stands in the Northeast corner of the lodge, to the Worshipful Master who presides in the East, together with all created intelligences, should with reverence, most humbly bow."

The Master and all the brethren bow; he gives one rap and the lodge is again seated.

The Master then repeats from memory, or reads from the Monitor, the following charge. If he prides himself on being a good worker he of course learns the charge by heart and repeats it without the book; but if he is dull, as many Worshipful Masters are, he reads it as best he can.

CHARGE OF A FELLOW CRAFT.

"My Brother: Being advanced to the second degree of Freemasonry, I congratulate you on your preferment.

"Masonry is a progressive moral science, divided

---

* App. note O, page 268.

into different degrees; and as its principles and mystic ceremonies are regularly developed and illustrated, it is intended and hoped that they will make deep and lasting impression on the mind."

It is unnecessary to recapitulate the duties which, as a Fellow Craft, you are bound to discharge. Your general good reputation affords satisfactory assurance, that you will not suffer any consideration to induce you to act in any manner unworthy of the respectable character you now sustain; but, on the contrary, that you will ever display the discretion, the virtue, and the dignity which become a worthy and exemplary Mason.

Our laws and regulations you are strenuously to support, and be always ready to assist in seeing them duly executed. You are not to palliate or aggravate the offences of your Brethren; but in the decision of every trespass against our rules, you are to judge with candor, admonish with friendship, and reprehend with justice.

The impressive ceremonies of this degree are calculated to inculcate upon the mind of the novitiate the importance of the study of the liberal arts and sciences, especially of the noble science of Geometry, which forms the basis of Freemasonry, and which, being of a divine and moral nature is enriched with the most useful knowledge; for while it proves the wonderful properties of nature, it demonstrates the more important truths of morality. To the study of Geometry, therefore, your attention is specially directed.

Your past regular deportment and upright conduct have merited the honor we have conferred. In your present character, it is expected that at all our assemblies you will observe the solemnities of our ceremonies, that you will preserve the ancient usages and customs of the Fraternity sacred and inviolate, and thus, by your example, induce others to hold them in due veneration.

Such is the nature of your engagements as a Fellow Craft, and to a due observance of them you are bound by the strongest ties of fidelity and honor.

"You will now be seated at the right of the Senior Warden in the West."

The foregoing ceremonies, together with the ceremonies used at opening and closing, constitute the second or Fellow Craft degree. As in the Entered Apprentice degree, so also in this—when a brother is *passed* he is turned over to some other brother to be posted; and having learned the ritual of the first section, he is afterward publicly examined in open lodge, and being found proficient and the ballot being found *clear,* he is ready to be *raised* to what is termed the "subiime" degree of a Master Mason.

CHAPTER VI.

The following questions and answers are Masonically termed "the lecture," and is that upon which the candidate must be closely examined before receiving the Master Mason's degree. Every stranger also who desires to visit, is examined on these lectures, and none will be allowed a seat in the lodge unless proficient in this catechism. The brother who has "posted" the candidate usually examines him as follows:

LECTURE.

Q. "Will you be off or from?"

A. "From."

Q. "From what to what?"

A. "From the degree of Entered Apprentice to that of Fellow Craft."

Q. "Are you a Fellow Craft?"

A. "I am, try me."

Q. "How will you be tried?"

A. "By the square."

Q. "Why by the square?"

A. "Because it is an emblem of morality and one of the working tools of a Fellow Craft."

Q. "What is a square?"

A. "An angle of ninety degrees or the fourth part of a circle."

Q. "What makes you a Fellow Craft?"

A. "My obligation."

Q. "Where were you made a Fellow Craft?"

A. "In a regularly constituted lodge of Fellow Crafts."

Q. "How were you prepared?"

A. "By being divested of all metals, neither naked nor clad, bare-foot nor shod, hood-winked and with a cable-tow twice around my naked right arm, in which condition I was conducted to the door of the lodge by a brother."

Q. "Why had you a cable-tow twice around your right arm?"

A. "To signify that as a Fellow Craft I was under a double tie to the fraternity."

Q. "How gained you admission?"

A. "By three distinct knocks."

Q. "What was said to you from within?"

A. "Who comes here?"

Q. "Your answer?"

A. "Bro. James Hunt, who has been regularly initiated as an Entered Apprentice and now seeks *more* light in Masonry by being passed to the degree of Fellow Craft."

Q. "What were you then asked?"

A. "If it was of my own free-will and accord; if I was worthy and well qualified, duly and truly prepared, and had made suitable proficiency in the preceding degree; all of which being answered in the affirmative I was asked by what further right or benefit I expected to gain admission?"

Q. "Your answer?"

A. "By the benefit of the pass."

Q. "Did you give the pass?"

A. "I did not, but my conductor gave it for me."

Q. "How were you then disposed of?"

A. "I was directed to wait with patience until the Worshipful Master was informed of my request and his answer returned?"

Q. "What answer did he return?"

A. "Let him enter in the name of the Lord and be received in due form."

Q. "How were you received?"

A. "On the angle of a square applied to my naked right breast, which was to teach me that the square of virtue should be the *rule* and *guide* of my conduct in all my future transactions with mankind."

Q. "How were you then disposed of?"

A. "I was conducted twice around the lodge to the Junior Warden in the South, where the same questions were asked and like answers returned as at the door."

Q. "How did the Junior Warden dispose of you?"

A. "He directed me to the Senior Warden in the West, and he to the Worshipful Master in the East, where the same questions were asked and like answers returned as before."

Q. "How did the Worshipful Master dispose of you?"

A. "He *ordered* me to be reconducted to the Senior Warden in the West, who taught me to approach the East by two upright regular steps, my feet forming the angle of a square, my body erect at the altar before the Worshipful Master."

Q. "What did the Worshipful Master then do with you?"

A. "He made me a Fellow Craft Mason in due form.

Q. "What is that due form?"

A. "Kneeling on my naked right knee, my left forming a square, my right hand resting on the Holy Bible, square and compass, my left arm forming a right angle supported by a square, in which due form I took upon myself the solemn oath or obligation of a Fellow Craft Mason, which is as follows." (See page 122.)

Q. "After taking the obligation what were you asked?"

A. "What I most desired."

Q. "Your answer?"

A. "More light in Masonry."

Q. "Did you receive more light in Masonry?"

A. "I did, by order of the Worshipful Master and the assistance of the brethren."

Q. "Upon being brought to light what did you discover more than before?"

A. "One point of the compass elevated above the square, which was to teach me that I had as yet received light in Masonry but partially."

Q. "What did you next discover?"

A. "The Worshipful Master approaching me from the East, under the due-guard and sign of a Fellow Craft, who, in token of the continuance of friendship and brotherly love, presented me with his right hand and with it the pass, token of the pass, grip and word of a Fellow Craft, ordered me to arise and salute the Junior and Senior Wardens as such."

Q. "After saluting the Wardens, what did you next discover?"

A. "The Worshipful Master, who ordered me to be re-conducted to the Senior Warden in the West, who taught me how to wear my apron as a Fellow Craft."

Q. "How should a Fellow Craft wear his apron?"

A. "With the bib turned down, and the left corner turned up in the form of a triangle."

Q. "After being taught how to wear your apron, how were you then disposed of?"

A. "I was reconducted to the Worshipful Master in the East, who presented me with the working tools of a Fellow Craft and taught me their uses."

Q. "What are the working tools of a Fellow Craft?"

A. "The plumb, square and level."

Q. "What are their Masonic uses?"

A. "The *plumb* is an instrument made use of by operative Masons to try perpendiculars; the *square* to square their work, and the *level* to prove horizontals; but we, as Free and Accepted Masons, are taught to make use of them for more noble and glorious purposes. The plumb admonishes us to walk uprightly in our several stations before God and man, squaring our actions by the square of virtue, and ever remembering that we are traveling upon the *level* of time to that undiscovered country, from whose bourne no traveler returns."

Q. "How were you then disposed of?"

A. "I was reconducted to the place whence I came, invested with what I had been divested of, and returned to the lodge, where in accordance with an ancient custom adopted in every regular and well governed lodge I made a regular advance through a porch, by a flight of *winding stairs,* consisting of three, five and seven steps, to a place representing the middle chamber of King Solomon's temple, where I received instructions relative to the wages and jewels of a Fellow Craft."

Q. "What are the wages of a Fellow Craft?"

A. "Corn, wine and oil, emblematical of the corn of nourishment, the wine of refreshment and the oil

of joy."

    Q. "What do they denote?"

    A. "Plenty, health and peace."

    Q. "What are the jewels of a Fellow Craft?"

    A. "The attentive, ear, the instructive tongue and the faithful breasts."

The examining brother then, whoever he may be, examines the candidate or visitor in the step and grips, as explained in pages 120-127, and which, of course, it is quite unnecessary to go through with here, after which the candidate is requested to repair to the ante-room, there to await the action of the lodge or "the will and pleasure of the Worshipful Master."

It must not be forgotten that on all occasions when a brother, whether an Apprentice, a Craftsman or a Master Mason, is entering or retiring from the lodge he must make the due-guard and sign of the degree on which the lodge is then open; and should he fail to do this, whether through ignorance or neglect, his attention is invariably called to it, either by the Master or some one of the Wardens.

As Freemasonry claims to be "a *conservator* as well as a *depository* of religion, science and art," and "includes within its circle almost every branch of polite learning" (see Past Grand Master Pierson's "Traditions of Freemasonry" page 14, and Sickel's "General Ahiman Reson," page 116), it may not be amiss to state that the second or Fellow Craft degree contains all the "science" and "art" to be found in the institution; and as the whole of the second degree is given word for word, in the preceding pages, the reader is respectfully referred to them for a knowledge of the "sciences" and "arts" which Freemasonry boastfully pretends to impart to its deluded votaries.

CHAPTER VII.

THIRD OR SUBLIME DEGREE OF MASTER MASON.

The ground-work of the third or "sublime" degree of Master Mason is based upon the pretended assassination of one Hiram Abiff, a mechanic of considerable celebrity who resided in the ancient city of Tyre, and whom Hiram, King of Tyre, sent to King Solomon to assist in the construction of the once famous temple at Jerusalem. The story of his mythical death is termed in the lodge, "the legend of the Tyrian artist." We are informed by what is called "Masonic tradition" that Solomon, King of Israel, Hiram, King of Tyre, and Hiram Abiff, entered into a solemn compact never to communicate the so-called Master's word until the temple was completed, and then only in the presence of the three, and that in consequence of his fidelity to his trust when attacked immediately before the completion of the temple by the three Fellow Craft ruffians, Jubela, Jubelo and Jubelum, to extort from him these so-called secrets, Hiram Abiff was slain, and hence the Master's word was lost and the real secrets of Freemasonry lay buried in oblivion, and were unknown to any portion of the human family for a period of four hundred and fifty years, or until the building of the second temple after the Babylonish captivity. The pretended secrets of Freemasonry, the word which is supposed to have been *lost,* is, according to Masonic teaching, the true name of God, and hence if Masonic tradition is to be relied upon, neither the people of God assembled at the temple dedication, nor the high priest who ministered in the Holy of Holies, nor Elijah, nor Elisha, nor Isaiah, nor any other of God's prophets or people, ever knew, or have now, any knowledge of the Almighty's real name, except those who go cable-towed and hood-winked into a Masonic lodge, seeking for "further light," and which is to be imparted to them (very often by an infidel or rum-seller) at the rate of from fifty to one hundred dollars a piece. But this entire story of the assassination of Hiram is a falsehood, a base fabrication; .and the foundation being a lie, surely the super-structure cannot possibly be that upon which any man can rely for salvation, or to which a Christian minister can consistently unite himself by extra-judicial oaths and sanguinary death penalties. In 1 Kings vii. 40, we read: "And Hiram made the lavers and the shovels and the basins. So Hiram *made an end of doing all the work* that he made King Solomon for the house of the Lord." Again, in 2 Chron. iv. 11; "And Hiram made the pots and the shovels and the basins. And Hiram *finished the work that he was to make for King Solomon for the house of the Lord."* Now, if Hiram Abiff *finished* all the work that he was to make, how is it possible that he could have been assassinated before the temple was completed?

This degree, notwithstanding its glaring inconsistencies and the innumerable evidences of its undoubted pagan origin, is, nevertheless, considered as the most important, as it is in reality the very summit of "Ancient Craft Masonry." It is from brethren of this degree that the rulers of the craft are selected, because (according to Masonic authority) "it is only from those who are capable of giving instruction that we can reasonably expect to receive it."

There is no difference, as has been already re-marked between a lodge of Apprentices, Fellow Crafts or Master Masons, except in the manner of placing the "altar lights"—the Holy Bible, Square and Compass; and new members, heedless of this distinction, are very apt to make the due-guard and sign of a Master Mason as a salute to the Worshipful Master when entering a lodge of an inferior degree; indeed, I have often seen the Master's sign made in a lodge of Apprentices. The jewels worn by the different officers are also the same in each of the three degrees, and for the information of the general reader, shall be here enumerated in their order: The Worshipful Master wears a square; a Past Master wears a compass opened on a quarter circle, sun in the center; Senior Warden, a level; Junior Warden, a plumb; Treasurer, cross keys; Secretary, cross pens; Senior Deacon, square and compass, sun in the center; Junior Deacon, square and compass, quarter moon in the center; Stewards, a cornucopia; Tyler, a sword, saber shape.

In addition to the jewels worn by the Wardens there is also placed on the pedestal in front of each a small column about eighteen inches high, the Senior Warden's being marked with a *level,* and the Junior Warden's with a *plumb.* When a lodge is opened in any of the degrees the Senior Warden "erects his column," or, in other words, places it standing on his pedestal in front of his chair, and lays it down when the lodge is closed or "called off," while the Junior Warden's column is always down, except when the lodge is "called from labor to refreshment." (See page 31.) It will be only necessary to remark further that none but Masters, Past Masters or Wardens are per-mitted to confer the degrees of Masonry; and although

a brother may have received the honorary degree of
Past Master in a chapter, yet if elected as Worshipful
Master of a Blue Lodge, he must, before installation,
be again invested with "the secrets of the chair."
With these introductory remarks I shall now proceed
to give in detail the exemplification of the *work* of the
Master Mason's degree.

We will suppose that the lodge is opened on the
second degree, and that our candidate, the "Rev. James
Hunt," has been examined as to his proficiency in "the
lecture" of that degree as detailed in the last chapter.
The lodge is then raised to the Master's degree, as
follows:

Worshipful Master (one rap): "Brother Senior
Warden, are you satisfied that all present are Master
Masons?"

Senior Warden (rising): "All present are not
Master Masons, Worshipful."

Worshipful Master (addressing any Fellow Craft
present): "Those below the degree of Master Mason will please retire."

Any brother present who has attained only to the
degree of Fellow Craft will now step in front of the
altar, make the customary salute (the due-guard and
sign of a Fellow Craft), and retire to the ante-room;
and as no one but Master Masons are allowed to
remain in and around the lodge room during *"work"*
on the third degree, Fellow Crafts must at this stage
of the proceedings entirely leave the building, unless
those who are waiting to receive the degree. The
Master's order being obeyed as above, the Senior Warden says:

Senior Warden (still standing): "All present are
Master Masons, Worshipful."

Worshipful Master: "Brother Senior Warden, it is my order that we now dispense with labor on the second degree and resume on the third for *"work,"* this you will communicate to your Brother Junior Warden in the South, and he to the brethren present, that all having due notice thereof may govern themselves accordingly."

Senior Warden (one rap): "Brother Junior Warden, it is the order of the Worshipful Master that we now dispense with labor on the second degree and resume on the third for *work.* This you will communicate to the brethren present for their government."

Junior Warden (three raps): "Brethren, it is the order of the Worshipful Master, communicated to me by way of the West, that we now dispense with labor on the second degree and resume on the third for *work.* Take due notice thereof and govern yourselves accordingly."

Worshipful Master: "Together, brethren."

All the members now looking to the East, in unison with the Master, make the due-guard and sign of a Master Mason. (See page 33.)

Worshipful Master: "Accordingly I declare Keystone Lodge, No. 639, duly at labor on the third degree of Masonry. Brother Junior Deacon, so inform the Tyler. Brother Senior Deacon, arrange the altar."*

The Junior Deacon informs the Tyler, as in the two preceding degrees; the Senior Deacon proceeds to the altar, elevates both points of the compass above the square, and retires to his seat.

Junior Deacon (facing the East): "The Tyler is informed, Worshipful."

---

* As to how a Master Mason's Lodge is regularly opened. See pp. 28 to 31.

The Worshipful Master gives one rap, seating the lodge.

WORK

Worshipful Master: "Brother Junior Deacon, you will ascertain if there are any candidates in waiting."

The Junior Deacon taking his rod proceeds to the altar, makes the due-guard and sign (see page 33) and retires to the ante-room, where he finds Brother James Hunt who has been examined in open lodge (as already stated), re-enters the lodge-room, makes the usual salute and reports: (Gives three raps.)

Junior Deacon: "Worshipful Master, Brother James Hunt, a Fellow Craft is in waiting and desires to be raised to the sublime degree of a Master Mason."

Worshipful Master: "Brother Junior Deacon, you will take with you the Stewards, retire, prepare and present the candidate for the third degree."

The brethren here mentioned make the usual salute, the due-guard and sign of this degree, and retire to the "preparation room."

Worshipful Master: "Brother Senior Deacon, you will attend to *all* alarms and take charge of the door."

*PREPARATION.

He is divested of all his clothing, his coat, **vest,** boots, stockings, cravat, collar, and finally his pants being taken off, he is given an old (and frequently) dirty pair of drawers to put on. Both legs of the drawers are turned up above the knees, thus making his knees, legs and feet bare; both arms of his shirt are

rolled up above the elbows, making both arms bare; both breasts of the shirt are turned back so as to make both breasts bare (if the shirt bosom be closed in front as many are now-a-days, it must be either taken off altogether or else turned, the back to the front; in very many instances I have seen the shirt entirely off). A hoodwink is carefully fastened over the eyes, and a rope called a cable-tow is wound three times

* For the meaning of the preparation, see "Master's Carpet," pp. 251-260.

around his body; an apron is tied on with the bib turned down as a Fellow Craft (see page 129), in which condition he is duly and truly prepared to be made a Master Mason; and being thus prepared, the Junior Deacon leads him to the door as before, upon which he gives "three loud and distinct knocks." The Master in the meantime calls the lodge to order, and the Senior Deacon rising to his feet reports:

Senior Deacon: "Worshipful Master, there is an alarm at the door of the preparation room."

Worshipful Master: "Brother Senior Deacon, attend to the alarm and report the cause."

The Senior Deacon taking his rod proceeds to the door of the preparation room upon which he also gives three loud and distinct knocks, opens the door and the following dialogue occurs:

Senior Deacon: "Who comes here?"

Junior Deacon: "Brother James Hunt, who has been regularly initiated as an Entered Apprentice, passed to the degree of a Fellow Craft, and now seeks further *light* in Masonry by being *raised* to the sublime degree of Master Mason."

Senior Deacon (looking at candidate): "Brother Hunt, is this of your own free-will and accord?"

Candidate: "It is."

Senior Deacon: "Brother Junior Deacon, is the candidate worthy and well qualified?"

Junior Deacon: "He is."

Senior Deacon: "Is he duly and truly prepared?"

Junior Deacon: "He is."

Senior Deacon: "Has he made a suitable proficiency in the preceding degrees?"

Junior Deacon: "He has."

Senior Deacon: "Who vouches for this?"

Junior Deacon: "A brother."

Senior Deacon: "By what further right or benefit does he expect to gain admission?"

Junior Deacon: "By the benefit of the *pass.*"

Senior Deacon: "Has he *the pass?*"

Junior Deacon: "He has it not, but I have it for him."

Senior Deacon: "Give me the pass."

The Junior Deacon approaches nearer to the door and whispers into the ear of the Senior Deacon the word *Tubal-Cain,* and again retires to the side of the candidate.

Senior Deacon: "The *pass* is right; you will await with patience until the Worshipful Master is informed of your request and his answer returned."

The Senior Deacon closes the door and returns to the front of the altar where he reports as follows:

Senior Deacon (making due-guard of Master Mason) "Worshipful Master, the alarm was caused by Brother James Hunt who has been regularly *initiated* as an Entered Apprentice, *passed* to the degree of Fellow Craft and now seeks *further light* in Masonry by being *raised* to the sublime degree of Master Mason."

Worshipful Master: "Brother Senior Deacon, is this of his own free-will and accord?"

Senior Deacon: "It is."

Worshipful Master: "Is the candidate worthy and well qualified?"

Senior Deacon: "He is."

Worshipful Master: "Is he duly and truly prepared?"

Senior Deacon: "He is."

Worshipful Master: "Has he made a suitable proficiency in the preceding degrees?"

Senior Deacon: "He has."

Worshipful Master: "Who vouches for this?"

Senior Deacon: "A brother."

Worshipful Master: "By what further right or benefit does he expect to gain admission?"

Senior Deacon: "By the benefit of the *pass.*"

Worshipful Master: "Has he *the pass?*"

Senior Deacon: "He has it not, but I have it for him."

Worshipful Master: "Give me the pass."

Senior Deacon: "Tubal-Cain" (aloud, and making the due-guard).

Worshipful Master: "The pass is right, since he comes endowed with all these necessary qualifications, it is my order that he enter this lodge in the name of the Lord, and be received in due form."

The Senior Deacon being provided with a pair of compasses, returns to the door which he opens without ceremony, and exclaims:

Senior Deacon (to Junior Deacon): "It is the order of the Worshipful Master that the candidate enter this lodge in the name of the Lord, and be received in due form."

*RITE OF INDUCTION.

The Junior Deacon takes the candidate by the arm and leads him into the lodge-room, halting him about six or eight feet inside the door, and the Senior Deacon standing immediately in front of him says:

Senior Deacon: "Brother Hunt, upon your first admission into a lodge of Masons *you were received on the point of a sharp instrument* pressing your naked

---

* For the origin of this ceremony see the "Master's Carpet," pp. 262-267.

left breast. Upon your first admission into a lodge of Fellow Crafts *you were received on the angle of a square* applied to your naked right breast, which at those times were explained to you. Upon your first admission into a lodge of Master Masons, I receive you on the points of the compass extending from your naked right to left breast which is to teach you that as the most vital parts of man are contained within the breasts, so are the most excellent tenets of our institution contained within the points of the compass, which are *friendship, morality* and *brotherly love.*"

*RITE OF CIRCUMAMBULATION.

He then hands the compass to the Junior Deacon, and taking the candidate by the right arm, conducts him *three times* around the lodge-room, always traveling with the course of the sun—that is from the West, or Senior Warden's station, by way of the North towards the East, and thence around by way of the South, and so on to the West again. While the candidate is thus being led around, on passing the three principal stations for the first time—that is South, West and East—the Junior Warden gives *one* loud rap, the Senior Warden *one,* and the Master *one.* On his second trip around the Junior Warden gives two raps in quick succession, the Senior Warden two, and the Master two; and on being led around for the third time, each of these officers gives three loud and distinct raps. It is important to observe that the Junior Warden in the South always leads off in giving the raps in all the degrees, followed by the Senior Warden in the West, and then by the Worshipful Master in the East.

As the candidate is being thus led on his symbolic

---
* For the meaning of this ceremony, see "Master's Carpet," pp. 268-272.

pilgrimage, the Master or Chaplain reads from the
first to the seventh verse of the twelfth chapter of
Ecclesiastes, as follows:

"Remember now thy Creator in the days of thy
youth, while the evil days come not, nor the years draw
nigh, when thou shalt say, I have no pleasure in them.
While the sun, or the light, or the moon, or the stars
be not darkened, nor the clouds return after the rain;
in the day when the keepers of the house shall tremble,
and the strong men shall bow themselves, and the
grinders cease because they are few, and those that
look out of the windows be darkened, and the doors
shall be shut in the streets, when the sound of the
grinding is low, and he shall rise up at the voice of the
bird, and all the daughters of music shall be brought
low; also when they shall be afraid of that which is
high, and fears shall be in the way, and the almond
tree shall flourish, and the grasshopper shall be a
burden, and desire shall fail; because man goeth to
his long home, and the mourners go about the streets;
or ever the silver cord be loosed, or the golden bowl be
broken, or the pitcher be broken at the fountain, or
the wheel broken at the cistern. Then shall the dust
return to the earth as it was: and the spirit shall return unto God who gave it.*

This reading is so timed that the last words are
pronounced just as the candidate is halted in front of
the Junior Warden's station. In some aristocratic
lodges, in cities and large towns where they can afford
the luxury of an organ, solemn music is substituted
for the reading. In some lodges, also, and especially
in small country towns, both the reading and music are
dispensed with altogether. After the candidate is

---

* "Standard Monitor," Cook, 1903, p. 42.

thus conducted three times around the lodge room, he is halted in front of the Junior Warden's station in the South, and the Senior Deacon giving three raps on the floor with the end of his rod, that officer rises to his feet and enquires:

Junior Warden: "Who comes here?"

Senior Deacon: "Brother James Hunt, who has been regularly initiated as an Entered Apprentice, passed to the degree of Fellow Craft, and now seeks *further* light in Masonry by being *raised* to the sublime degree of a Master Mason."

Junior Warden (to candidate): "Brother Hunt, is this of your own free-will and accord?"

Candidate: "It is."

Worshipful Master: "Brother Junior Deacon, is the candidate worthy and well qualified?"

Senior Deacon: "He is."

Junior Warden: "Is he duly and truly prepared?"

Senior Deacon: "He is."

Junior Warden: "Has he made a suitable proficiency in the preceding degrees?"

Senior Deacon: "He has."

Junior Warden: "Who vouches for this?"

Senior Deacon: "A brother."

Junior Warden: "By what further right of benefit does he *expect to obtain this favor?*"

Senior Deacon: "By the benefit of the pass."

Junior Warden: "Has *he the* pass?"

Senior Warden: "*He* has it not, but I have it for him."

Junior Warden: "Give me the pass."

The Senior Deacon approaches a few paces nearer to the Junior Warden and whispers into his ear the word, "*Tubal-Cain.*"

Junior Warden: "The pass is right. You will conduct the candidate to the Senior Warden in the West for further examination."

The candidate is now conducted towards the West, and being halted in front of the Senior Warden's station, the Senior Deacon gives three distinct raps as before with the end of his rod, calling that officer to his feet; and precisely the same questions are asked, and the same answers returned, as at the Junior Warden's station, which it is not necessary to repeat again, and at the end of which the Senior Warden says:

Senior Warden: "The pass is right. You will conduct the candidate to the Worshipful Master in the East, for his examination."

He is then led towards the East, and again halted in front of the Worshipful Master's chair, where, as before, the Senior Deacon gives three distinct raps. The Master keeping his seat and in a very stern voice demands:

Worshipful Master: "Who comes here?"

Senior Deacon: "Brother James Hunt, who has been regularly initiated as an Entered Apprentice, passed to the degree of Fellow Craft, and now seeks further light in Masonry by being raised to the sublime degree of Master Mason."

Worshipful Master: "Brother Hunt, is this of your own free-will and accord?"

Candidate: "It is."

Worshipful Master: "Brother Senior Deacon, is the candidate worthy and well qualified, duly and truly prepared?"

Senior Deacon: "He is."

Worshipful Master: "Has he made a suitable proficiency in the preceding degrees?"

Senior Deacon: "He has."

Worshipful Master: "Who vouches for this?"

Senior Deacon: "A brother."

Worshipful Master: "By what further right or benefit does he expect to obtain this favor?"

Senior Deacon: "By the benefit of the *pass*."

Worshipful Master: "Has *he* the pass?"

Senior Deacon: "He has it not, but I have it for him."

Worshipful Master: "Give me the pass."

The Senior Deacon, as in the two previous cases, whispers into his ear the word, "Tubal-Cain."

Worshipful Master: "The pass is right. Since he comes endowed with all these necessary qualifications, it is my order that you re-conduct him to the Senior Warden, in the West, who will teach him to approach the East by three upright, regular steps, his feet forming the angle of a square, his body erect at the altar before the Worshipful Master."

The Senior Deacon now leads the candidate back, by way of the South, to the Senior Warden's station, before whom he is again halted, and the Deacon, giving one rap, addresses that officer as follows:

Senior Deacon: "Brother Senior Warden, it is the order of the Worshipful Master that you teach the candidate to approach the East by three upright, regular steps, his feet forming the angle of a square, his body erect at the altar before the Worshipful Master."

Senior Warden: "Brother Junior Deacon, you will face the candidate in the East." (standing up) "Brother Hunt, you will take the Entered Apprentice step—*step off one step with your left foot,* bringing the heel of the right to the hollow of the left. (The candidate is instructed how to perform the exceedingly scientific feat.) You will take the Fellow Craft step —*step off one step with your right foot,* bringing the heel of your left to the hollow of the right. (He is again instructed in this step.) You will now take one advance step with your left foot, and bring the heel of your right right foot *to the heel* of the left, your feet forming the angle of a square. (The Deacon places the candidate's feet as directed.) Stand erect. In order, Worshipful."

Worshipful Master (three raps: addressing candidate, see fig. p. 68) "Brother Hunt, you are now at the altar of Masonry for the third time; but before proceeding further, it becomes my duty, as the Worshipful Master of this lodge, to inform you that it will be necessary that you take upon yourself a solemn oath or obligation pertaining to this degree. And *I can assure you, upon the honor of a man and a Mason, that in this obligation there is nothing that will conflict with any duty, you owe to God, your country your family, your neighbor or yourself.* In your advancement thus far you have repeatedly assured us it was of your own free-will and accord; if you are still of the same mind, you will advance to our altar. (The Senior Deacon leads the candidate towards the altar.) Kneel on your *naked* knees, your hands resting on the Holy Bible, square and compass. (The Senior Deacon places the candidate as directed and stands at his left side.)"

---

* App. note B. B., p. 269.

*RITE OF SECRECY.

The Master now gives three raps, calling up the entire lodge. They all then approach the altar, and arrange themselves in two rows—one on either side of the altar and kneeling candidate, the ranks extending from West to East. The Master also approaches the altar, and, standing in front of the candidate, removes his hat and says:

Worshipful Master (continuing): "In which due form you will say "I," with your name in full, and *repeat after me:*

MASTER MASON'S OBLIGATION.

"I, James Hunt, of my own free-will and accord, in the presence of Almighty God and this Worshipful lodge, erected to him and dedicated to the Saints John,

do hereby and hereon (the Master at these words places his right hand upon those of the candidate) most solemnly and sincerely promise and swear:

"That I will always hail, ever conceal and never

* For the origin and meaning of this ceremony, see "Master's Carpet," pp. 373-379.

reveal any of the secret arts, parts or points of the Master Mason's degree to any person or persons whomsoever except it be to a true and lawful brother of this degree or within a regularly constituted lodge of Master Masons, and neither unto him nor them until by strict trial, due examination or legal information, I shall have found him or them as lawfully entitled to the same as I am myself.

"I furthermore promise and swear, that I will conform to, and abide by, all the laws, rules and regulations of the Master Mason's degree, and of the lodge of which I shall hereafter become a member, and that I will ever maintain and support the constitution, laws and edicts of the Grand Lodge under which the same shall be holden, so far as the same shall come to my knowledge.

"Furthermore, that I will answer and obey all due signs and summons sent to me from Master Masons' Lodge, or given me by a brother of this degree, if within the length of my cable-tow.

"Furthermore, that I will keep the secrets of a worthy brother Master Mason as inviolable as my own, when communicated to and received by me as such, murder and treason excepted.*

"Furthermore, that I will aid and assist all worthy distressed brother Master Masons, their widows and orphans, I knowing them to be such, so far as their necessities may require and my ability will permit without material injury to myself or family.

"Furthermore, that I will not assist in, or be present at, the initiating, passing or raising of a woman, an old man in dotage, a young man under age, an atheist, a madman or a fool, I knowing them to be such.

---

* Giving testimony against a brother Mason in Court which oath is to be obeyed? This or the legal oath?

"Furthermore, that I will not sit in a lodge of clandestine Masons, nor converse upon the secrets of Freemasonry with a clandestine Mason, nor with one who
is under the sentence or expulsion or suspension, to
my knowledge, while under such sentence.

"Furthermore, that I will not knowingly strike a
brother Master Mason, nor otherwise do him personal
violence in anger, except it be in the necessary defense
of my person, family or property.

"Furthermore, that I will not cheat, wrong nor
defraud a Master Mason Lodge, nor a brother of
this degree, nor supplant him in any of his laudable
undertakings, but will give him due and timely notice,
that he may ward off approaching danger, if in my
power.

"Furthermore, that I will not have illicit carnal
intercourse with a brother Master Mason's wife, his
mother, sister or daughter, I knowing them to be such,
nor suffer it to be done by others, if in my power to
prevent it.

"Furthermore, that I will not give the Grand Hailing sign or sign of distress of a Master Mason unless
in real distress, or in cases of the most imminent
danger, in a regularly constituted lodge of Master
Masons, or in a secure place for Masonic instruction;
and should I see the sign given or hear the words accompanying it, I will repair to the relief of the person
so giving it, if there is a greater probability of saving
his life than of losing my own.*

"Furthermore, that I will not give the Grand
Masonic word in any other manner or form than
that in which I shall hereafter receive it, and then
only in low breath.

"All this I most solemnly and sincerely prom-

---

* Will a Masonic juror obey this or his legal oath? Which?

ise and swear with a firm and steadfast resolution to keep and perform the same without any equivocation, mental reservation, or secret evasion of mind whatever, *binding myself under a no less penalty than that of having my body severed in twain, my bowels taken from thence and burned to ashes, and the ashes scattered to the four winds of heaven, that no trace or remembrance may be had of so vile and perjured a wretch as I,* should I ever knowingly violate this my solemn obligation as a Master Mason. So help me, God, and keep me steadfast in the due performance of the same.

Worshipful Master (to candidate): "In token of your sincerity, you will detach your hands and kiss the Bible."

The candidate's hands are removed by the Senior Deacon, and he stoops down and kisses the book.

Worshipful Master (to Senior Deacon): "Brother Senior Deacon, you will release the brother from the cable-tow he is bound to us by an obligation, a tie stronger than human hands can impose."

The Deacon removes the cable-tow from around the candidate's body and throws it aside. The Worshipful Master now resumes his hat and steps back a few paces, always facing the candidate, the Stewards or Deacons cross their rods, over the Master's head, and in this position he continues:

*THE RITE OF ILLUMINATION.

Worshipful Master: "Brother Hunt, in your present condition what do you most desire?"

Candidate (prompted by Senior Deacon): "Further light in Masonry."

Worshipful Master: "Brother Senior Deacon and brethren, you will assist me in bringing this brother from darkness to light. 'In the beginning God created the heavens and the earth, and the earth was without form and void, and darkness was upon the face of the deep. And the spirit of God moved upon the face of the waters. And God said, Let there be light, and there was light.' In humble commemoration of which august event, we Masonically say, 'Let there be light.'" (See fig. p. 71.)

Here the Senior Deacon swiftly removes the hoodwink from the candidate's eyes, the Worshipful Master and brethren standing on either side make the due-guard of a Mason, as on page 39, and retaining their hands in this position for a few seconds, the Master remarks:

Worshipful Master: "And there is light."

Worshipful Master (approaching the candidate): "My brother, upon being brought to light in this degree, you discover the *three great lights* in Masonry, as before, with this difference, both points of the compass elevated above the square, which is to teach you never to lose sight of the Masonic application of that useful and valuable instrument which teaches *friendship, morality* and *brotherly love.*"

The Worshipful Master then steps back eight or ten paces and the Senior Deacon, addressing the candidate, says:

Senior Deacon: "You now behold the Worshipful Master approaching you from the East under the due-guard (Master makes the due-guard of a Master Mason, as on page 33) and sign of a Master Mason. (Worshipful Master makes the penal sign, see figure page 34.)"

Worshipful Master (to candidate): "An Entered Apprentice steps off with his left foot, bringing the heel of the right to the hollow of the left forming the angle of a square (he makes his step). A Fellow Craft steps off, with his right foot, bringing the heel of the left to the hollow of the right, forming also the angle of a square (Master also makes this step), and these are the first and second steps in Masonry. A Master Mason steps off with his left foot, bringing the heel of the right to the heel of the left, forming the angle of a square (makes this step), and this is the third step in Masonry. This was given you as the due-guard, and this as the sign of an Entered Apprentice. (Master makes the due-guard and sign of the first degree, see figures, page 16.) This was given you as the due-guard and this as the sign of a Fellow Craft which at those times were explained to you (he now makes the due-guard and sign of the second degree, see figures, pages 27-28). This is the due-guard (making the due-guard of a Master Mason, as on page 33) and alludes to the position in which your hands were placed while taking your obligation. This is the sign (makes the penal sign of a Master Mason, as on page 34) and alludes to the penalty of your obligation."

*RITE OF INTRUSTING.

Worshipful Master (approaching candidate): In token of the further continuance of friendship and brotherly love, I present you my right hand (takes the candidate by the right hand), and with it the *pass* and *token of the pass* of a Master Mason; but as you

---
* For the meaning of this ceremony, see "Master's Carpet," pp. 287-291.

are uninstructed, I will explain them with Brother Senior Deacon. Take me as I take you (pressing his thumb hard on the second knuckle of the candidate's right hand, the candidate does the same)."

Worshipful Master: "Brother Senior Deacon, will you be off or from?"

Senior Deacon (standing at right side of candidate): "From."

Worshipful Master: "From what to what?"

Senior Deacon: "From the real grip of a Fellow Craft to the pass-grip of a Master Mason."

Worshipful Master: "Pass."

The Senior Deacon, now removes the candidate's thumb to the space between the second and third knuckles of the Master's right hand, while the Master moves *his* thumb to the corresponding space on the candidate's hand. (See figure.)

Worshipful Master: "What is this? (pressing hard with his thumb)."

Senior Deacon: "The pass grip of a Master Mason."

Worshipful Master: "Has it a name?"

Senior Deacon: "It has."

Worshipful Master: "Will you give it to me?"

Senior Deacon: "I did not so receive it, neither will I so impart it."

Worshipful Master: "How will you dispose of it?"

Senior Deacon: "I will syllable it with you."
Worshipful Master: "Syllable and begin.
Senior Deacon: "No, you begin."
Worshipful Master: "You .iust begin."
Senior Deacon: "Bal."
Worshipful Master: "Tu."
Senior Deacon: "Cain."
Worshipful Master: "Tubal."
Senior Deacon: "Tubal-Cain."

Worshipful Master (looking at candidate) : "The name of this grip, is Tubal-Cain. Tubal-Cain was the first inventor of curious smith-work and of metalic operations by fire, and was the eighth man from Adam. You will now arise and salute the Junior and Senior Wardens as a Master Mason." *

The Master then steps to the East, resumes his gavel, gives one rap and the lodge is seated. In some lodges the Senior Warden stands in the West during the entire ceremony from the time the candidate kneels at the altar; and when the Master has concluded his remarks about Tubal-Cain he gives the rap which seats the lodge.

The Senior Deacon now conducts the candidate by way of the East to the Junior Warden in the South and that officer rising to his feet, both he and the Senior Deacon and candidate make the step, due-guard and sign of a Master Mason. He is then led to the Senior Warden, and that officer also rising, the step, due-guard and sign are again made by all three. The candidate is then re-conducted slowly towards the East, and as he arrives on a line with the altar the Worshipful Master gives one rap, halting both the Deacon and candidate, and enquires:

---

* "They have gone in the way of Cain," Jude 11.

Worshipful Master (one rap): "How is it in the South, Brother Junior Warden?"

Junior Warden (rising): "All right in the South, Worshipful."

Worshipful Master (one rap): "How is it in the West, Brother Senior Warden?"

Senior Warden (rising): "All right in the West, Worshipful."

Worshipful Master (one rap): (to Senior Deacon) "Brother Senior Deacon, you will re-conduct the brother to the Senior Warden in the West, who will teach him how to wear his apron as a Master Mason."

The candidate should now be led directly back to the Senior Warden's station without passing around the altar; but some deacons, not being well posted, lead him around by way of the South, and standing in front of the Senior Warden the Deacon addresses him as follows:

Senior Deacon: "Brother Senior Warden, it is the order of the Worshipful Master that you teach the brother how to wear his apron as a Master Mason."

*RITE OF INVESTITURE.

Senior Warden: "My brother, Masonic tradition informs us that at the building of King Solomon's Temple, Master Masons wore their aprons with the corner turned down in the form of a square to designate them as Master Masons or overseers of the work. As a speculative Master Mason you will therefore wear yours in this manner to admonish you that your action toward all mankind should possess the qualities of that perfect figure to symbolize the in-

---

* For the origin and meaning of this rite, see "Master's Carpet," pp. 292-297.

tegrity of your service to God, and to remind you of your four fold duty to your country, your family, your neighbor and yourself."

The Senior Warden takes his seat; the Senior Deacon re-conducts the candidate to the East and leaves him standing in front of the Master's chair, while he himself returns to his usual place. The Worshipful Master, rising to his feet, takes a small trowel and looking at candidate says:

Worshipful Master: "As you are now clothed as a Master Mason you are now entitled to your

WORKING TOOLS.

"The working tools of a Master Mason are all the implements of Masonry indiscriminately, but more especially the trowel. The trowel is an instrument made use of by operative Masons to spread the cement which unites the building into one common mass; but we as Free and Accepted Masons are taught to make use of it for the more noble and glorious purpose of spreading the cement of brotherly love and affection— that cement which unites us into one sacred band or society of friends and brothers, among whom no contention should ever exist, but that noble contention, or rather emulation, of who best can work and best agree."*

"You will now be reconducted to the place whence you came, invested with what you had been divested of and await the further will and pleasure of the Worshipful Master."

This latter clause, or words of similar import, are put in by the Worshipful Master to deceive the candidate, and to throw him off his guard by conveying the impression that the entire ceremonies of the degree

---

"Standard Monitor." Cook. 1903 p. 43-4.

are now over, and that nothing more remains to be done except to put on his clothes and go home.

The Senior Deacon conducts the candidate to the altar where he makes the usual salute, the due-guard and sign, and is taken in charge by the Junior Deacon or Stewards who lead him back to the preparation-room and assist him to dress.

And thus the first section or Initiary Ceremonies of this sublime degree are concluded.

The third degree, like the first, is divided into three sections. The first section comprises all that part of the degree from the "preparation" to the return of the candidate to the ante-room; the second section is that part where the *death, burial* and *raising* of Hiram are represented, and is regarded as the most important and sublime portion of the whole Masonic ritual; and the third section comprises "the historical record" of the degree, "the emblems" and the "charge."

SECOND SECTION.

When the candidate in company with the Junior Deacon and stewards retires into the ante-room to resume his clothing, the lodge is usually called from "labor to refreshment," and while it is thus "called off," active preparations are being made for working the second section or dramatic portion of this degree. The Senior Deacon procures a strong canvass, kept in every lodge for the purpose, about eight feet long and five feet wide, ordinarily furnished with three loops on each side by which it can be firmly held, also a pretty large, round substance made of india-rubber with a short wooden handle, and called by Masons a "setting maul;" he then brings out a small wooden box about eighteen inches long. eight inches wide and twelve inches high, containing a gong in the inside of it, and which is operated by a spring on the top. The "setting maul" and "canvass" on such occasions are usually placed under or near the Treasurer's desk, but so hidden that the candidate cannot see them, on re-entering the lodge, and the small wooden box (masonically termed a *low twelve bell*) is placed near the Master's chair. The three *ruffians* or those who are to kill poor *Hiram* are also appointed at this stage of the proceedings, as are also the Fellow Crafts who are to do most of what is termed the *floor work,* and all other necessary preparations are made to correctly represent the murder of "our Grand Master Hiram Abiff."

When the candidate is dressed the Junior Deacon suspends from his neck a small plumb attached to a blue ribbon, and which is known as the Junior Warden's jewel; he also ties on an apron worn in the usual manner with the bib and corners turned down, and being thus clothed he is conducted into the lodge-room, where he is warmly congratulated by the Worshipful Master, Wardens and brethren, and various other little demonstrations manifested to make it apparent to the candidate that the degree is finished and that he has passed through the trying ordeal with more than ordinary courage and firmness. After a few moments being thus spent in this silly little bit of by-play the candidate is placed sitting in the Junior Warden's chair and the Master taking his seat, and, giving one rap, "calls on" the lodge and all is ready for proceeding with the really interesting part of the "sublime" degree of Master Mason.

Worshipful Master: "Brother Senior Deacon, you will conduct Brother Hunt to the East."

All being on the tip-toe of expectation, the Worshipful Master addressing candidate, says:

Worshipful Master: "My brother, I suppose you now consider yourself a Master Mason? I presume you do from the jewel you wear. However natural this supposition may be to you, it is erroneous. You are not yet a Master Mason so far as to enable you to prove yourself one or to travel and work as a Master Mason. The impressive ceremonies which are to follow and in which you are to take an important part are intended to impress on the mind of the candidate the solemn and binding character of the obligations he has taken and to symbolize the vital and fundamental truth of the immortality of the soul and the life beyond the grave. You have a rough and rugged road to travel, beset with ruffians and may be with murderers, and should you lose your life in the conflict yours will not be the first. My brother remember in whom you put your trust 'he that endureth unto the end the same shall be saved.' In a preceding degree, you had some one to pray for you, but now you must pray for yourself. You will therefore suffer yourself again to be *hood-winked,* kneel where you are, and pray, either mentally or orally as you choose, when done you will say 'Amen,' arise and make your progress.

The Senior Deacon now steps forward and again places a hoodwink securely over the candidate's eyes and causes him to kneel on both knees as it were to pray, but in the whole course of my Masonic experience I never knew the candidate to pray. The Worshipful Master stands up, removes his hat and gives three raps, calling all the brethren to their feet, and thus standing they await for some minutes till the candidate says "Amen" aloud.

The figures on next page correctly represents this portion of the ceremony.

And should the candidate delay too long in saying "Amen" either the Deacon or Master whispers in
his ear, "Say Amen aloud," and he repeating "Amen"
the Master says to him:

Worshipful Master: "You will now arise and
make your progress." (One rap.)

The candidate, representing Hiram Abiff, is now
assisted to his feet by the Senior Deacon who conducts
him in the usual manner once around the lodge-room,
and says:

Senior Deacon: "My brother, heretofore in
your progress in Masonry, you have been a candidate
in search of Masonic light. You now represent our

Brother Hunt praying for himself.

Grand Master Hiram Abiff, who was Grand Architect at the building of King Solomon's Temple and was slain just before its completion. Our Grand Master Hiram Abiff was slain at high twelve, while the craft were called from labor to refreshment it being his custom at that hour to enter into the unfinished sanctum sanctorium or Holy of Holies of the temple to offer up his devotions to Deity and draw his designs on the trestle board. This you have done. The day of his assassination he was about to return at the South gate as you will now do. As he approaches the South or Junior Warden's station he is rudely accosted by one of the brethren previously appointed to represent *Jubela* or the first *ruffian,* who catches him by both collars of the coat and vest, shakes him roughly, and says:

Jubela: "Grand Master Hiram, I am glad to meet you thus alone; this is an opportunity I have long sought. You know you promised us that when the temple was completed we should receive the secrets of a Master Mason, or the Master's word, whereby we might travel in foreign countries, work and receive Master's wages: behold the temple is well-nigh completed and we have not obtained that for which we so long sought, I therefore demand of you the secrets of a Master Mason."

Senior Deacon (for candidate): "My brother, this is an unusual way of asking for the secrets of a Master Mason, neither is it a proper time nor place; you keep your promise and I will keep mine. Wait until the temple is completed, when if found worthy, you will doubtless receive them, otherwise you cannot."

Jubela (shaking candidate rather roughly): "Talk not to me of time nor place; at first I did not doubt your veracity, but now I do. Give me the secrets of a Master Mason."

Senior Deacon: "I *shall* not, neither *can* they be given until the temple is completed, and then only in the presence of three: Solomon, king of Israel; Hiram, king of Tyre; and myself."

Jubela (shaking and pushing candidate about still more violently): "I'll have no more of your parley; give me the secrets of a Master Mason or the Master's word, or I will take your life."

Senior Deacon: "I *will* not."

Jubela draws the twenty-four inch gauge swiftly across his throat,* then attempts to pass out of the West gate.

Jubelo (shaking candidate with some violence):

---

*For the meaning of this pretended attack and murder, see "Master's Carpet" pp. 355-368.

"Grand Master Hiram, give me the secrets of a Master Mason."

Senior Deacon (for candidate): "I cannot."

Jubelo (still more angrily): "Give me the secrets of a Master Mason."

Senior Deacon: "I shall not."

Jubelo (shaking candidate with greater violence): "Give me the secrets of a Master Mason or the Master's word, or I'll take your life."

Senior Deacon: "I will not."

Jubelo: (He strikes him a slight blow with the square across the left breast, then attempts the East gate.)

Six brethren are now beckoned forward to the northeast corner of the lodge, close to the Treasurer's desk, where they procure the *canvass* before mentioned, open it out, taking hold of it by the loops, and the candidate being very swiftly hurried towards the East, he is met by the *third ruffian, Jubelum,* who catches him by both collars, as before, and wheels him around so as to bring his heels to the edge of the canvass held by the brethren, when he says:

Jubelum (shaking canvass with more violence than

did any of the others): "Grand Master Hiram, give me the secrets of a Master Mason."

Senior Deacon (for candidate): "I cannot."

Jubelum. "Jubela and Jubelo you have evaded, but me you cannot escape. My name is Jubelum. What I purpose that I perform. Give me the secrets of a Master Mason."

Senior Deacon: "I shall not."

Jubelum (taking setting maul and touching candidate's forehead with the short wooden handle) : "In my hand I hold an instrument of death, with which if you do not give me the secrets of a Master Mason or the Master's word, I'll take your life in an instant."

Senior Deacon: "I will not."

Jubelum (to candidate) : "Die then."

At the same time he strikes him a smart blow with the pretended "setting maul" on the forehead and gives him a strong push which causes him to fall backward into the canvass, as seen in the figure, page 186.

The candidate is then laid on his back on the floor, covered up with the canvass, and all the brethren retire to their seats, except the three supposed *ruffians.*

Jubela (in astonishment) : "What horrid deed is this we have done?"

Jubelo: "We have murdered our Grand Master, Hiram Abiff, and have not obtained that for which we have so long sought."

Jubelum (in greater astonishment): "Is he dead?"

Jubela: "He is (putting his hand on candidate's forehead), his skull is broken."

Jubelo: "Well, this is no time for reflection; what shall we do with the body?"

Jubelum (in terror) : "Let us bury it in the rubbish of the temple until low twelve (twelve at night) when we three will meet and give it a more decent burial."

Ruffians (together): "Agreed."

The canvass containing the candidate is then lifted up by six of the brethren and carried across the room to the southeast corner near the Secretary's desk, where he is again laid down and frequently covered up with chairs, pieces of wood, etc., as seen on page 189, to represent the rubbish of the temple, and all again retire to their seats except the *three ruffians.* Jubelum, seating himself near the candidate, says to his two companions:

Jubelum: "Now I will stay here and watch while you two go and dig a grave, after which we will meet and bury it "

The two ruffians, Jubela and Jubelo, move off towards the Senior Warden's station where they pretend to be digging a grave, the lights are all turned down to represent night, that is, provided gas is used in the lodge-room, and the Master sitting in the East begins to strike very slowly and at equal intervals twelve strokes on the "low twelve bell," representing midnight. As the hours of ten and eleven are being struck the *ruffians,* Jubela and Jubelo, approach the supposed dead body where the watching and expectant Jubelum rises up and says:

Jubelum: "Is that you, Jubela? "
Jubela: "Yes."
Jubelum: "Is that you, Jubelo? "
Jubelo: "Yes."
Both together: "Is that you, Jubelum?
Jubelum: "Yes, low twelve and we are not yet discovered. Now what shall we do with the body? "
Jubela: "Let us convey it a westerly course from the temple to the brow of a hill west of Mount Moriah where we have been and dug a grave due East and West, six feet perpendicular, and there bury it."

EAST.

Rev. Dr. Hunt playing dead where
he falls into the canvas.

Rev. Dr. Hunt "buried under the
rubbish of the temple" with
Jubelum watching.

Rev. Dr. Hunt buried in front of
Senior Warden's station at the
foot of an acacia tree.

WEST.

For the meaning of this figure see "Master's Carpet", pp. 344-385.

Jubelo and Jubelum: "Agreed."

The canvass and body are again lifted up and borne on the shoulders of the brethren towards the West, where it is deposited in front of the Senior Warden's station, having the head towards the West and the feet towards the East, and all but the three ruffians take their seats as before. Jubelum, taking the Senior Warden's column, says:

Jubelum: "Let us plant this acacia in the head of the grave (he places the little column standing at the candidate's head) to conceal it and that the place may be known should occasion ever require it. Now let us make our escape."

This whole ceremony of the death, concealment and burial of Hiram is correctly represented on the foregoing page. The *ruffians* then pass out by way

of the "preparation-room" door, and after a few minutes delay re-enter the lodge by the door of the ante-room, inside of which they find the Junior Deacon carelessly lounging and who represents a sea captain at the port of Joppa, where the fugitive ruffians are now supposed to be.

Jubelum (to Junior Deacon): "Halloo! are you a sea captain?"

Junior Deacon (as sea captain): "I am."

Jubelum: "Are you going to put to sea soon?"

Junior Deacon: "I am, tomorrow."

Jubela: "Whither are you bound?"

Junior Deacon: "To Ethiopia."

Jubelum (addressing his companions): "The very place we wish to go; (turning to Junior Deacon) here are three of us, can we get a passage with you?"

Junior Deacon: "You can. I shall be pleased with your company. You have King Solomon's pass, I presume?"

Jubelum (in derisive astonishment): "King Solomon's pass, no! We came away in a hurry and on urgent business and must go. We did not suppose a pass would be necessary. We have plenty of money (putting his hand in his vest pocket) and will pay you any price you ask."

Junior Deacon: "There is an embargo laid on all the shipping, and if you have not King Solomon's pass you cannot get a passage with me, neither can you from this port."

Jubelum (to his companions): "Well, I suppose we have to go back and get a pass."

Junior Deacon: "The sooner the better, you are suspicious looking characters."

They now move off, and approaching the spot where the body is lying, the following colloquy takes place:

Jubela (to his companions): "Well, what shall we do now?"

Jubelo: "Let us steal a boat and put to sea."

Jubela: "Agreed."

Jubelum: "Ho! that will not do. This is an iron-bound coast and we shall be thrown against the rocks and dashed to pieces."

Jubela: "Well, what shall we do?"

Jubelo: "Let us flee to some other port."

Jubela: "Agreed."

Jubelum: "Ho! that will not do; before we can arrive at another port the whole coast will be lined with our pursuers and we shall be taken and executed."

Jubelo (in despair): "Well, what *shall* we do?"

Jubelum (pausing a few seconds): "Let us flee into the mountains and secrete ourselves as well as we can and preserve our lives as long as we can."

Jubela and Jubelo: "Agreed."

They then pass hurriedly from the lodge room into the preparation room where they seat themselves to await future developments. The Master now slips out quietly into the ante-room and all the members begin to talk loud, sing, whistle, walk about, etc., creating a general confusion, in the midst of which the Worshipful Master re-enters the lodge, representing King Solomon, and in many so-called aristocratic lodges, clothed in a scarlet robe trimmed with white fur and wearing a head-dress resembling a crown. On entering the lodge he struts forward, aping the manners of a king, and giving one heavy blow with his gavel on the Junior Warden's pedestal, he exclaims:

Worshipful Master (as King Solomon): "Brother Senior Grand Warden, what is the cause of all this confusion, why are not the craft pursuing their labors?" *

Senior Warden (rising): "Most Excellent King Solomon, there are no designs on the trestle board."

Worshipful Master (in astonishment): "No designs on the trestle board? Where is our Grand Master Hiram Abiff?"

Senior Warden: "He has not been seen since high twelve yesterday."

Worshipful Master (in greater astonishment): "Not been seen since high twelve yesterday! I fear he is indisposed. Let strict search and due inquiry be made for him in and about the several apartments of the temple and see if he can be found."

Senior Warden (three raps): "Craftsmen, let strict search and due enquiry be made in and about the several apartments of the temple and see if our Grand Master Hiram Abiff can be found."

Here brethren ask aloud, "Have you seen our Grand Master Hiram Abiff? He's not been seen since high twelve yesterday."

Senior Warden (one rap): "Most Excellent King Solomon, strict search and due inquiry have been made, in and about the several apartments of the temple and our Grand Master Hiram Abiff cannot be found."

Worshipful Master (sorrowfully): "I fear some fatal accident has befallen him. (Turning to Secretary) "Brother Grand Secretary, let the several rolls of the workmen be called." (The Master retires to his seat.)

The Secretary takes a long strip of paper on

---

* This confusion and alarm is to represent that consternation, which, according to the legend, prevailed in Egypt when the god Pan bore the intelligence to the Egyptians of the death of Osiris, and hence our word panic

which he has written some Scriptural names, and going towards the ante-room he calls out, "Craftsmen assemble—assemble for roll call." Some of the brethren, twelve if possible, now retire into the ante-room, and the Secretary proceeds in a loud voice to call the roll as follows:

Secretary (calling roll): "Abraham," some brother responds) "Here;" Adoniram," "Here;" Ammishadai," "Here;" "Jubela,"—no response; "Jubela, Jubela;" Jethro," "Here;" "Josephus," "Here;" "Jediah," "Here;" "Jubelo,"—no response; "Jubelo, Jubelo;" "Benjamin," "Here;" "Bezaleel," "Here;" "Belshazar," ' Here;" "Jubelum,"—no reply; "Jubelum, Jubelum;" "Tebulim," "Here; "Tephaniah," "Here;" "Tedekiah," "Here."

Having thus called the roll he re-enters the lodge-room, leaving the door partly open, approaches the altar and making the due-guard of a Fellow Craft,* reports:

Secretary: "Most Excellent King Solomon, the several rolls of the workmen have been called as ordered, and three Fellow Crafts are missing, namely: Jubela, Jubelo and Jubelum, who from the similarity of their names are supposed to be brethren and men of Tyre."

Just then three loud and distinct knocks are sounded on the door from the outside, and the Secretary, still standing at the altar, reports further:

Secretary (making due-guard as before): "Most Excellent King Solomon, there are without twelve Fellow Crafts, who say they have important tidings to communicate."

---

* The reader will observe that in working this second section of the Master's degree all present except the Worshipful Master and Senior Warden are supposed to be Fellow Crafts, and hence the due-guard of a Fellow Craft is always made in addressing

Worshipful Master: "You will admit them."

Junior Deacon (opening the door): "Enter, you twelve Fellow Crafts."

The brethren in the ante-room now enter the lodge and marching straight to the East, arrange themselves in a line in front of the Master's chair when one of their number who is well posted, becomes spokesman and makes the following report: (all make due-guard.)

1st Fellow Craft (making due-guard): "Most Excellent King Solomon, fifteen of our Fellow Crafts seeing the temple about to be completed and being desirous of receiving the secrets of a Master Mason or Master's word, whereby we might travel in foreign countries, work and receive Master's wages, entered into a horrid conspiracy to extort them from our Grand Master Hiram Abiff, or take his life. But, reflecting with horror on the atrocity of the crime, twelve of us have recanted.* The other three, we fear have persisted in their murderous design. We therefore appear before your Majesty, clad in white gloves and aprons (extending his hands), in token of our innocence, acknowledge our premeditated guilt and most humbly implore your pardon."

They all kneel upon the left knee, at the same time making the due-guard of a Fellow Craft.

Worshipful Master: "Arise, you twelve Fellow Crafts, and divide yourselves into parties and travel three East, three West, three North, and three South, with others whom I shall appoint *in search* of the *ruffians,* and return not without tidings."

All except the three best posted brethren, whom I

* For the origin of this number 12, see "Master's Carpet," p. 366.
† For the origin of this search, see "Master's Carpet," pp. 353-354.

shall designate as Fellow Crafts Nos. 1, 2, 3, now take their seats, and these proceeding very slowly in their pretended search of the *ruffians* pass out by the "preparation-room" door, and after a short delay enter the lodge-room again by the ante-room door, supposed to be the port of Joppa, inside of which they meet the Junior Deacon as before, when the following dialogue takes place:

2nd Fellow Craft (in search of the ruffians): "Halloa, friend! Have you seen any strangers pass this way?"

Wayfaring Man (he is generally the Junior Deacon, at the port of Joppa): "I have; three."

2nd Fellow Craft: "What sort of appearing men were they?"

Wayfaring Man: "They appeared to be workmen from the temple and men of Tyre, seeking a passage into Ethiopia; but not having King Solomon's pass they could not obtain a passage and turned back into the country."

2nd Fellow Craft (addressing his companions): "These are doubtless the very men we are in search of. (Turning to Wayfaring Man) You say they turned back into the country?"

Wayfaring Man: "They did."

2nd Fellow Craft (to his companions): "Now let us go up and report this intelligence to King Solomon."

They now proceed to the East, and standing in front of the Master's chair, Fellow Craft No. 2 makes the following report:

Fellow Craft No. 2 (makes due guard of Fellow Craft): "Most Excellent King Solomon, tidings."

Worshipful Master: "Report."

Fellow Craft No. 2: "We being of the party who pursued a westerly course, on coming down near the port of Joppa, fell in with a wayfaring man, of whom we inquired if he had seen any strangers pass that way. He informed us that he had, three; who from their appearance were workmen from the temple and men of Tyre, seeking a passage into Ethiopia, but not having your pass, they could not obtain a passage and turned back into the country."

Worshipful Master: "These are doubtless *the ruffians.* It is my order that you disguise yourselves and travel as before with positive injunctions to find the ruffians, and with as positive assurance that if you do not, you twelve Fellow Crafts shall be deemed the murderers and severally suffer for the crime committed. Depart (gives a loud rap with his gavel as if angry)."

The three Fellow Crafts now travel as before in search of the supposed *ruffians,* proceeding slowly towards the "preparation-room" door, and spending more time than usual outside, they again enter the lodge-room by the ante-room door and approaching the spot where the candidate, representing the murdered and buried *Hiram,* is all this time lying, the following conversation takes place between them:

Fellow Craft No. 3: "Well, here we are back in sight of the temple. It will not do for us to go up and report, for if we do the poor Fellow Crafts will be executed."

Fellow Craft No. 1: "Let us take a Southwesterly or a Northwesterly course."

Fellow Craft No. 2: "Well, I am tired. I am going to sit down and rest and refresh myself."

Fellow Craft No. 3: "O, Come along, we may as

well go up and report ourselves and suffer the penalty of our conspiracy."

And suiting the action to the word he seats himself near the candidate's head.

The other two Fellow Crafts move off a little way, going very slowly and as it were arranging what route they shall take next, when one of them looks back and beckoning to him who is sitting down says:

The weary Fellow Craft now in attempting to arise catches hold of the Warden's column, representing an *acacia* as before mentioned, and pretending to pull it up by the roots stumbles a little in rising, looks at the supposed *acacia* in astonishment and exclaims:

Fellow Craft No. 2: "Hold, companions! (they turn around and walk back hurriedly). On attempting to arise I accidentally caught hold of this *acacia*, which easily giving way excites my curiosity. Let us look around here. This has the appearance of a new-made grave."

Just as the word "grave" is pronounced the three pretended *ruffians*, Jubela, Jubelo and Jubelum, supposed to be hiding in the clefts of an adjacent rock, and who for the time being are sitting immediately inside the door of the "preparation-room," now utter the following exclamations, the three Fellow Crafts, in the meantime, intently listening and commenting upon each exclamation as it is made:

Jubela: "Oh, that my *throat had been cut across, my tongue torn out by its roots and buried in the rough sands of the sea at low water-mark, where the tide ebbs and flows twice in twenty-four hours,* ere I had been accessory to the death of so *great* a man as our Grand Master Hiram Abiff!"

Fellow Craft No. 1 (to his companions in a low

tone): "Listen, that's the voice of Jubela."

Jubelo: "Oh, that *my left breast had been torn open, my heart plucked out and given as a prey to the beasts of the field and the fowls of the air* ere I had consented to the death of so *good* a man as our Grand Master Hiram Abiff!"

Fellow Craft No. 2 (as before): "That is the voice of Jubelo."

Jubelum: "Oh, that *my body had been severed in twain, my bowels taken from thence and burned to ashes and the ashes scattered to the fourwinds of heaven, that no trace or remembrance might be had of so vile and perjured a wretch as I,* ere I had *caused* the death of so great and so good a man as our Grand Master Hiram Abiff! Ah! Jubela and Jubelo, it is I who am more guilty than you both; it was I who gave the fatal blow, it was I who killed him."

Fellow Craft No. 3 (excitedly): "That is the voice of Jubelum; they are confessing their guilt. What shall we do?"

Fellow Craft No. 1: "Let us rush in, seize, bind, and take them before King Solomon."

Fellow Craft No. 2: "But they are desperate men."

Fellow Craft No. 3: "Well, we have truth and justice on our side; let us rush in."

All: "Agreed."

They then make a sudden rush for the "preparation-room" where a sharp and short scuffle is supposed to take place between the pursuers and pursued, and in a little while the three Fellow Crafts again enter the lodge-room, each one leading a pretended murderer as prisoner, whom they march up to King Solomon (Worshipful Master) and cause to kneel in front of the Master's chair. The following report is then made:

Fellow Craft No. 3 (making due-guard of Fellow Craft) : "Most Excellent King Solomon, we being of the party which pursued a westerly course a second time, were returning after several days fruitless search when one brother being more weary than the rest sat down at the brow of a hill west of Mount Moriah to rest and refresh himself, on attempting to arise he accidentally caught hold of an *acacia* which easily giving way excited his curiosity. Whereon he hailed his companions, and on our return and examination, we found the appearance of a newly-made grave. While meditating on this singular circumstance we heard the following horrid exclamations from the clefts of an adjacent rock. The first was the voice of Jubela, who exclaimed, 'Oh, that my throat had been cut across, my tongue torn out by the roots,' etc. (as already given.) The second was the voice of Jubelo, who exclaimed, 'Oh, that my left breast had been torn open, my heart plucked out,' etc. And the third was the voice of Jubelum, who exclaimed in tones of greater horror than the others, 'Oh, that my body had been severed in twain, my bowels taken from thence,' etc., whereon we rushed in, seized and bound them and now have them before your Majesty (pointing to the kneeling ruffians)."

Worshipful Master (addressing ruffians) : "What have you to say, Jubela, are you guilty?"

Jubela: "Guilty, Most Excellent King Solomon."

Worshipful Master: "Are you guilty, Jubelo?"

Jubelo: "More guilty, Most Excellent King Solomon."

Worshipful Master: "What have you to say, Jubelum. Are you guilty or not guilty?"

Jubelum: "Most guilty, Most Excellent King Solomon."

Worshipful Master (very sternly): "Vile miscreants and infamous wretches that you are. You have murdered your Grand Master Hiram Abiff and have not obtained that for which you so long sought. Reflect on the atrocity of your crime and on the amiable and exemplary character of him whom you have so basely assassinated. Hold up your heads and receive your sentence. (The three kneeling persons hold up their heads and look at the Master.) It is my order that you be taken without the gates of the city, *and there executed according to your several imprecations* while in the clefts of the rock. (Addressing the Fellow Crafts) Guards, away with them. (Gives a loud rap and pretends to be very angry.)"

The ruffians are now marched very slowly back again into the "preparation-room" where they are supposed to be slain according to the strict injunction of King Solomon, and which is usually done in the following manner: The Fellow Crafts having the ruffians in charge, balance three times with the right hand and right leg; the third time stamping the right foot on the floor and striking the palm of the right hand against the palm of the left. This they do three times and the pretended execution is over, affording considerable mirth to those outside and often forcing a delicate smile from the brethren in the lodge. The three Fellow Crafts now return to the East and one of them making the due-guard as usual, reports:

Fellow Craft No. 3: "Most Excellent King Solomon, your orders have been duly executed."

Worshipful Master: "It is now my order that you twelve Fellow Crafts go in search of the body of our Grand Master Hiram Abiff; and if found to observe whether the Master's word or a key to it or anything appertaining to the Master's degree is on or about it."

They move away very slowly towards the Senior Warden's station, where the candidate is all this time lying, and as they go, Fellow Craft No. 3, asks:

"Where is that weary brother who sat down to rest and refresh himself?"

Fellow Craft No. 2: "Here I am."

Fellow Craft No. 3: "Do you think you can find the place?"

Fellow Craft No. 2: "I think I can (stepping forward towards the candidate's head and picking up the little column before referred to). Here is the *acacia* and here is the place."

Fellow Craft No. 3: "Let us dig down and see what we can find."

The candidate up to this time has been snugly covered up in the *canvass,* and this they now roll back which in the scientific language of Masonry means "digging down." and having come to the supposed body they spread their hands over the pretended grave in the manner of the due-guard of a Master Mason. (See figure, page 203.)

Fellow Craft No. 1: "This is the body of our Grand Master Hiram Abiff."

Fellow Craft No. 2: "What was it King Solomon ordered us to do?"

Fellow Craft No. 3: "To observe whether the Master's word or a key to it or anything appertaining to the Master's degree was on or about the body."

Fellow Craft No. 1: "What do we know about the Master's word or a key to it? We are only Fellow Crafts"

Fellow Craft No. 2: "True, but we must obey orders."

Fellow Craft No. 3: "Well, let us examine and see what we can find.*"

The three Fellow Crafts now begin to fuss and fumble about the candidate's body, pretending to search on his person for the *lost word* or key to the secrets of a Master Mason, and after a few seconds thus spent Fellow Craft No. 1 laying hold of the miniature *plumb* suspended from the candidate's neck as already mentioned, he enquires in some astonishment: (See Figure.)

Fellow Craft No. 1: "What is this?"

Fellow Craft No. 2 (also handling the plumb): "That must be the jewel of his office."

Fellow Craft No. 3: "Let us take this (the jewel) and go up and report, and if King Solomon says nothing about the Master's word or a key to it we won't."

Fellow Crafts (together): "Agreed."

One of the supposed Fellow Crafts now removes the pretended jewel from around the candidate's neck and they again proceed to King Solomon's throne-room

* For the origin of this second search, see "Master's Carpet," pp. 346, 347.

(the Master's chair), where the following report is made by the third Fellow Craft:

Fellow Craft No. 3 (making due-guard): "Most Excellent King Solomon, tidings from the body."

Worshipful Master (representing King Solomon): "Report."

Fellow Craft No. 3: "The body of our Grand Master Hiram Abiff was found a Westerly course from the temple in a grave dug due East and West, six feet perpendicular in the brow of a hill where our weary brother sat down to rest and refresh himself."

Worshipful Master: Was the Master's word or a key to it or anything appertaining to the Master's degree found on or about it?"

Fellow Craft No. 3 (making due-guard): "Most Excellent King Solomon, what do we know of the Master's word or the key to it, we are only Fellow Crafts."

Worshipful Master: "True."

Fellow Craft No. 3: "Nothing was found but this jewel of his office by which the body was designated (handing the little *plumb* to the master), the jewel of his office."

Worshipful Master: "Present it" (receiving the plumb and rising to his feet) "This is indeed the jewel of our Grand Master Hiram Abiff. It is now my order that you twelve Fellow Crafts form in procession and go and assist in raising the body; and as the Master's word is now lost I propose my worthy companion of Tyre that the first sign given on arriving at the grave and the first word spoken after the body shall be raised shall be adopted as the sign and word for the regulation of all Master's lodges until future generations shall find out the right."

All Fellow Crafts: "Agreed."

The Worshipful Master then gives three raps which call all the brethren to their feet, and they proceed to the supposed grave standing in a circle around where the candidate is lying. The Master also approaches the pretended prostrate Hiram, and as he arrives at the feet of the candidate the Senior Warden slips the hoodwink from his eyes. The Worshipful Master then spreads his hands over the supposed grave in the manner of the due-guard of a Master Mason (see figure, page 33) the rest of the brethren doing the same, and then they all raise their hands perpendicularly above their heads and let them fall by three distinct motions. Oh Lord, My God, is there no help for the Widow's Son. (This is the grand hailing sign or sign of distress of a Master Mason, and is more fully explained on page 209.) The Master now proceeds to the head of the grave, the Senior Warden being on his right hand and the Junior Warden on his

* For the origin and meaning of this, see "Master's Carpet."
p. 373.

left, and they all march three times slowly around the grave of the prostrate candidate, singing as they go the following funeral dirge to the tune of Pleyel's hymn :

"Solemn strikes the funeral chime,
Notes of our departing time,
As we journey here below
Through a pilgrimage of woe.

"Mortals now indulge a tear,
For mortality is here.
See how wide her trophies wave
O'er the slumbers of the grave.

"Here another guest we bring;
Seraphs of celestial wing,
To our funeral altar come,
Waft our friend and brother home.

"There enlarged thy soul shall see
What was veiled in mystery.
Heavenly glories of the place
Show his maker face to face.

Lord of all ! below—above,
Fill our hearts with truth and love;
When dissolves our earthly tie,
Take us to thy Lodge on high." *

The singing of this hymn, br a portion of it, is sc timed that at least the first, second and last stanzas are concluded by the time the Master arrives at the head of the grave the third time, when the procession is halted all the brethren standing around the body

* The two first verses and the last verse are generally used, "Standard Monitor," Cook, 1902, p. 45.

as before.   The Worshipful Master then addresses
one of the brethren, usually the Junior Warden, as
follows:

Worshipful Master: "It is now my order that
one of you twelve Fellow Crafts take the body by the
Entered Apprentice grip and see if it can be raised."

The Junior Warden, now steps forward to the
right side of the candidate and taking him by the right
hand presses the top of his thumb hard against the
first knuckle joint of the fore-finger next the hand.
(See figure, page 74.)   He also lays hold of his right
arm above the elbow firmly with his left hand, and
holding the candidate thus he pretends to put forth
very great exertion in attempting to pull him out of the
supposed grave, or in Masonic parlance to *raise* him
by the "Entered Apprentice grip" and after one long
vigorous effort he forcibly slips his hand from that
of the candidate and reports as follows:

Fellow Craft No. 3 (making the due-guard):
"Most Excellent King Solomon, owing to the high
state of putrefaction, the body having been dead
already fifteen days, *the skin slips* and it cannot be so
raised."

The Worshipful Master and all the brethren now
raise their arms perpendicularly above their heads and
let them fall by three distinct motions, at the same
time exclaiming, "Oh Lord my God, is there no help
for the Widow's Son?"   (This is the *grand hailing
sign or sign of distress.*   See figure, page 209.)

Worshipful Master (addressing Senior Warden):
"My worthy companion of Tyre, you will now take
the body by the Fellow Craft's grip and see if it can
be so raised."

The Senior Warden now steps forward and takes

hold of the candidate's right hand and arm as the Junior Warden had done, at the same time pressing his thumb hard against the *second knuckle* of the right hand which is the Fellow Craft grip (see figure, page 142), and bracing himself firmly as the previous brother did he makes another vigorous effort to raise the body as before, but permits his hand to slip off as in the former case, and reports:

Senior Warden (making due-guard): "Most Excellent King Solomon, owing to the reasons already assigned, *the flesh cleaves from the bone* and the body cannot be so raised."

The Worshipful Master and all the brethren again raise their hands perpendicularly and let them fall by three distinct motions as before, at the same time exclaiming, "Oh Lord my God, I fear the Master's word is forever lost!"

In order to understand more distinctly how this sign is made and the exclamation given, I will here offer the following explanation: It will be remembered that the arms when raised perpendicularly are to be let fall by *three distinct* motions. The exclamation is also divided into *three distinct* parts with a slight pause between each, thus: "Oh Lord—my God—is there no help for the Widow's Son?" Or, "Oh Lord —my God—I fear the Master's word is forever lost!" In letting the arms fall you make the first motion and give the first part of this exclamation, "O Lord," together. This brings the arms from the shoulder to the elbow in a horizontal position and the fore-arms perpendicular, as seen in figure. Now drop the arms by another motion, still holding the hands in an upright position and repeat the second part of the exclamation, "My God," and lastly let the hands fall perpendicularly to the side, using the third part of the exclamation, "Was there no help for the Widow's

Grand Hailing
Sign—Second
Position.

Son?" or, "I fear the Master's word is forever lost!" Thus it will be seen that the first motion and first part of the exclamation are made together, the second motion and second part together, and the third motion and third part together. For the manner of giving the sign outside the lodge, see pages 214-215.

Worshipful Master (turning to Senior Warden): "My worthy companion of Tyre, what shall we do?"

Senior Warden (representing Hiram, king of Tyre): "Let us pray."

All the brethren now kneel on one knee around the candidate, and the Master removing his hat repeats the following so-called

PRAYER:

"Thou, O God! knowest our downsitting and our uprising and understandeth our thoughts afar off. Shield and defend us from the evil intentions of our enemies and support us under the trials and afflictions

we are destined to endure while traveling through this vale of tears. Man that is born of woman is of few days and full of trouble. He cometh forth as a flower and is cut down; he fleeth also as a shadow and continueth not. Seeing his days are determined, the number of his months are with thee: thou hast appointed his bounds that he cannot pass; turn from him that he may rest till he shall accomplish his day. For there is hope of a tree if it be cut down that it will sprout again and that the tender branch will not cease. But man dieth and wasteth away: yea, man giveth up the ghost and where is he? As the waters fail from the sea and as the flood decayeth and drieth up so man lieth down and riseth not up until the heavens shall be no more. Yet, O God, have compassion upon the children of thy creation, administer them comfort in time of trouble and save them with an everlasting salvation. Amen."

Response by the brethren, "So mote it be."

They all now stand up and the Master resuming

his hat again spreads his hands over the supposed grave (the candidate) as in the due-guard of a Master Mason (see figure, page 39) and exclaims:

Worshipful Master: "I now command perfect silence. And with your assistance, my worthy companion of Tyre (to Senior Warden), I will now raise the body by the strong grip of a Master Mason or the "lion's paw." *

The Master then steps forward and taking the candidate by the right hand—grasping it firmly—presses the tops of his fingers very strongly against the joint of the candidate's wrist where it unites with the hand, the candidate pressing his fingers against the corresponding part of the Master's hand and the space between the thumb and first finger of each being interlocked. (This is a very firm grip and is called the "strong grip of a Master Mason" or "lion's paw." See figure.) The Master also with his left hand lays hold of the candidate's right arm near the shoulder, while the Senior Warden takes him by the left arm and then both Master and Senior Warden exerting considerable force they lift him to his feet, on

"THE FIVE POINTS OF FELLOWSHIP."

This is done by the Master still retaining his grasp of the candidate's right hand, and placing the inside of

* For the true meaning and origin of the "lion's paw," as well as the raising of Hiram, see "Master's Carpet," pp. 377-390.

his right foot against the inside of the right foot of the candidate, the toe of the one being towards the heel of the other, his right knee against the candidate's

right knee, the right breast of the one close against the right breast of the other, the Master's left hand against the candidate's back and the candidate's left hand against the Master's back, also the Master's right cheek against the right cheek of the candidate, or the mouth of the one to the ear of the other, as in the annexed figure: the Worshipful Master then whispers into his ear the word, *Mah-hah-bone,* at the same time instructing the candidate to whisper the same word into his (the Master's ear), which he does. They then release each other and the Master steps back a few paces, while the Senior Warden gives one rap which seats all the brethren, leaving the Master, candidate, and Senior Deacon standing on the floor together.

The foregoing ceremony is called *raising,* and in connection therewith the following is frequently proposed by Masons as a sort of "catch" or test question to try strangers:

"*From* what, *to* what, *by* what and *on* what were you made a Master Mason?" Answer:

"*From* a dead level *to* a living perpendicular; *by* the strong grip of a Master Mason or "lion's paw," *on* the Five Points of Fellowship."

Worshipful Master: "My brother, you have now been raised by the strong grip of a Master Mason or the 'lion's paw,' (See Master Mason's obligation, pages 170-173) on the 'Five Points of Fellowship,' which are *foot to foot, knee to knee, breast to breast, hand to back, cheek to cheek* or mouth to ear.

"*Foot to foot,* teaches that you will ever go on foot and out of your way to assist a needy, worthy brother.

"*Knee to knee;* that in all your devotions to Deity you will remember a brother's welfare as well as your own.

"*Breast to breast;* that you will ever keep within your breast the secrets of a worthy brother Master Mason as inviolable as your own when communicated to, and received by you as such, murder and treason excepted.

"*Hand to back;* that you will ever stretch forth your hand to save a falling brother, and that you will vindicate his character behind his back as well as before his face.

"*Cheek to cheek,* or mouth to ear; that you will ever whisper good counsel in the ear of an erring brother; and in the most friendly manner remind him of his errors and aid in his reformation; and that you will give him due and timely notice that he may ward off approaching danger, if in your power.

"The word which I have just given you is the word adopted for the regulation of all Master Mason

Lodges, until future generations shall find out the right and is that word which you have solemnly sworn never to give in any other manner or form than that in which you have received it and then only in low breath.

"I will now further explain to you the signs pertaining to this degree. This, you will remember, was given you as the due-guard (makes the due-guard) and this as the sign of a Master Mason (makes the sign, see figure, page 34). They, have a further allusion. Our ancient brethren on arriving at the grave of our Grand Master Hiram Abiff involuntarily placed their hands in this (makes again the due-guard) or this position (places the right hand as in figure 2, page 34, at the same time averting the face a little toward the right shoulder) to shield their nostrils from the offensive effluvia that assailed them from the grave."

See scene at the grave, page 203.

"This is the *grand hailing sign or sign of distress* of a Master Mason (see figure, also page 209) raising your hands up in this manner (he raises both hands perpendicularly above his head) and letting them fall three times (he drops his hands as indicated); and is that sign which you have solemnly sworn never to give unless in real distress, or in cases of the most imminent danger, in a regularly constituted lodge of Master Masons or in a secure place for Masonic instruction.' (See obligation, page 170.) Should you be in distress, you will give this sign three times, Master Mason observing it will repair to your relief if there is a greater probability of saving your life than of losing his own, and should you see the sign given your obligation will be the same. The words substituted for this sign in the dark or at other times, when it cannot be given are, 'O Lord, my God, is there no help for the Widow's Son?' and are equally as binding on you as though you had the sign given. These also have a further allusion: Our ancient brethren raising the body of our Grand Master Hiram Abiff, in token of horror and surprise at the mangled conditions of the body, raised their hands above their heads (he raises his hands perpendicularly as already explained) and exclaimed, 'O Lord, my God, is there no help for the Widow's Son?'"

"I will now further explain the grips pertaining to this degree. 'Take me as I take you.'"

Taking candidate by the right hand as in ordinary hand-shaking, he presses his thumb hard against the space between the second and third knuckles, the candidate returning a like pressure on the Master's hand. (See figure, page 176.) "This, you will remember, is the *pass-grip* of a Master Mason. We get from this by saying:"

Worshipful Master: "Brother Deacon, will you be off or from?"

Senior Deacon (answering for candidate): "From."

Worshipful Master: "From what to what?"

Senior Deacon: "From the pass-grip of a Master Mason to the true grip of the same."

The Master now quits his hold of the candidate's

knuckles and grasping his right hand more firmly, with the thumbs of both interlaced, he presses the tops of his fingers against the wrist of the candidate where it unites with the hand, the candidate at the same time being instructed to press his fingers against the corresponding part of the Master's hand and the fingers of each being somewhat apart. See figure.

Worshipful Master (to Senior Deacon): "Pass —What is this?"

Senior Deacon (for candidate): "The strong grip of a Master Mason or the Lion's Paw."

Worshipful Master: "Has it a name?"

Senior Deacon: "It has, it being that which I have solemnly sworn never to give in any other manner or form than that in which I have received it, and then only in low breath."

Worshipful Master: "Will you give it to me?"

Senior Deacon: "I will if you place yourself in a proper position to receive it."

Worshipful Master: "What is that position?"

Senior Deacon: "Foot to foot (Master and candidate extend their right feet, placing the inside of one against that of the other); knee to knee (they bring their right knees together); breast to breast

Five Points of
Fellowship.

(they bring their right breasts together); hand to back (Master places his left hand on the candidate's back, the candidate's is placed by the Deacon, on the Master's back); check to check or mouth to ear (Master puts his mouth to candidate's right ear thus bringing the right cheek of each together. See figure, page 216)."

The Worshipful Master then whispers in the ear of the candidate the word *Mah-hah-bone,* after which the candidate whispers the same word in the Master's ear.

This is the only manner in which this word can be given whether in the lodge-room or out of it. (See obligation, page 171.)

Worshipful Master (addressing candidate): "You will now repair to the East and receive a historical account of this degree."

The Master here gives one rap, and seats the lodge and retires to his seat and the Senior Deacon, conducting the candidate towards the East, places him in front of the Master's chair where he is permitted to sit or stand as the Worshipful Master sees fit until the remaining section of the degree is concluded.

This closes the "legend of the Tyrian artist," or the dramatic part of the "sublime degree of Master Mason" and comprises those ceremonies in which the brethren feel the deepest interest and which they are the most anxious to witness of all the degrees in Freemasonry. In many lodges in Chicago the foregoing ceremonies are conducted with great exactness and imposing solemnity, the requisite number of members in each lodge being thoroughly drilled so that each one can correctly perform his own part in the drama. This is especially the case in all lodges."

THIRD SECTION.

The only preparation necessary for working the third section of this degree is to place the "Master's chart," or as it is sometimes called, the "Master's carpet," in a conspicuous place in front of the candidate, so that he may be enabled to see the various figures displayed thereon whenever referred to by the Worshipful Master in the course of the ensuing "lecture." It may also be proper to remark that the "Master's chart" or "carpet" is a painting either on canvass or paper, and on which is delineated the different hieroglyphical emblems peculiar to this degree; such as the *three steps,* the *pot of incense,* the *bee-hive,* etc., etc. Some of these emblems have already been alluded to in the preceding sections; the others will be fully' explained according to the *standard work* in the section which is now to follow.

THE LEGEND OF HIRAM ABIFF.

Worshipful Master (to candidate): "My brother, you have this evening represented one of the greatest men, if not *the* greatest man and Mason that ever lived, no less a man than our ancient Grand Master Hiram Abiff who was slain just before the completion of the temple.*

"His death being premeditated by fifteen Fellow Crafts, who seeing the temple about to be completed and being desirous of receiving the secrets of a Master Mason or the Master's word whereby they might travel in foreign countries, work and receive Master's wages, entered into a horrid conspiracy to extort them from our Grand Master Hiram Abiff or take his life.

---

* For the true origin and meaning of this legend, see the "Master's Carpet," pp. 344-376.

But reflecting with horror on the atrocity of the crime twelve of them recanted; the other three, still, however, persisted in their murderous design.

"Our Grand Master Hiram Abiff was slain at *high twelve* while the craft were called from labor to refreshment. It being his custom at that hour to enter into the unfinished 'sanctum sanctorum' or 'Holy of Holies' of the temple, there to offer up his devotion to the Deity and draw his designs on the trestle-board. The three Fellow Crafts who persisted in their murderous design knowing this to be his usual practice placed themselves at the South, West and East gates of the inner court of the temple and there awaited his return. Our Grand Master Hiram Abiff having finished his usual exercises was about to retire at the South gate, where was accosted of the *first ruffian,* who thrice demanded of him the secrets of a Master Mason or Master's word and on his refusal he gave him a blow with the *twenty-four-inch gauge* across his throat on which he fled and attempted to pass out of the West gate where he was in like manner accosted by the *second,* who thrice demanded of him the secrets of a Master Mason or the Master's word, and in a like refusal he gave him a blow with a *square* across his breast. Whereupon he fled and attempted to escape by the East gate where he was likewise accosted by the *third,* who thrice demanded of him the secrets of a Master Mason or the Master's word, and on a similar refusal he gave him a violent blow with a *setting maul* on his forehead which felled him dead on the spot.

"They then buried the body in the rubbish of the temple until *low twelve* or twelve at night, when they met by appointment and conveyed it a westerly course from the temple to the brow of a hill west of Mount Moriah, where they had been and dug a grave due East and West, six feet perpendicular, and there buried it. In the head of the grave they planted an accacia to conceal it and that the place might be known should occasion ever require and made their escape.

"Our Grand Master Hiram Abiff was found to be missing on the day following, from there being no designs on the trestle-board. King Solomon being informed thereof, at first supposed him to be indisposed, and ordered strict search and due inquiry to be made for him in and about the several apartments of the temple. Strict search and due inquiry were accordingly made, but he could not be found. King Solomon then fearing that some fatal accident had befallen him ordered the several rolls of the workmen to be called.

"At roll-call three Fellow Crafts were found to be missing, namely, *Jubela, Jubelo* and *Jubelum,* who from the similarity of their names were supposed to be brethren and men of Tyre.

"At this time the twelve Fellow Crafts who had recanted from their murderous designs appeared before King Solomon, clad in white gloves and aprons, in token of their innocence, acknowledged their premeditated guilt and most humbly implored his pardon. King Solomon then ordered the twelve Fellow Crafts to divide themselves in parties and travel three East, three West, three North and three South (with others whom he should appoint), *in search of the ruffians* and return not without tidings. They traveled and at the point while pursuing a westerly course coming down near the port of Joppa, they fell in with a *way-*

faring man of whom they *enquired* if he had seen any strangers pass that way. He informed them that he had three, who from their appearance were workmen from the temple and men of Tyre seeking a passage into Ethiopia, but not having King Solomon's pass could not obtain a passage and turned back into the country. They returned and reported this intelligence to King Solomon, who ordered them to disguise themselves and travel as before with positive injunctions to find the ruffians and with as positive assurance that if they did not the twelve Fellow Crafts should be deemed the murderers an severally suffer for the crime committed. They traveled and as the party which pursued a westerly course a second time were returning after several days fruitless search, one brother being more weary than the rest sat down at the brow of a hill west of Mount Moriah to rest and refresh himself. On attempting to arise he *accidentally caught hold of an acacia* which easily giving way excited his curiosity, whereupon he hailed his companions, and on their return and examination, they found the appearance of a newly made grave. While meditating on this singular circumstance they heard the following horrid exclamations from the clefts of an adjacent rock. The first was the voice of *Jubela*, who exclaimed, 'Oh, that my throat had been cut across, my tongue torn out by its roots and buried in the rough sands of the sea at low water mark, where the tide ebbs and flows twice in twenty-four hours, ere I had been accessory to the death of *so great* a man as our Grand Master Hiram Abiff!' The second was the voice of *Jubela*, who exclaimed, 'Oh, that my left breast had been torn open, my heart plucked out and given as a prey to the beasts of the fields and

the fowls of the air, ere I had *consented* to the death
of *so good* a man as our Grand Master Hiram Abiff!'
The third was the voice of *Jubelum,* who exclaimed in
tones of greater horror than the others, 'Oh, that my
body had been severed in twain, my bowels taken from
thence and burned to ashes and the ashes scattered to
the four winds of heaven, so that no trace or remembrance might be had of so vile and perjured a wretch
as I, ere I had *caused* the death of *so great* and *so
good* a man as our Grand Master Hiram Abiff! Ah,
Jubela and *Jubelo,* it is I who am more guilty than
you both; it was I who gave the fatal blow, it was
I who killed him!' whereupon they rushed in, seized
and bound them and took them before King Solomon,
who after a due confession of their guilt ordered them
to be taken without the gates of the city and there
executed according to their several imprecations, in
the clefts of the rock. They were taken out and
executed accordingly.

"King Solomon then ordered that the twelve Fellow Crafts *go in search* of the body of our Grand
Master Hiram Abiff and if found to observe whether
the Master's word or a key to it or anything appertaining to the Master's degree were on or about it.
The body of our Grand Master Hiram Abiff was
found in a westerly course from the temple in a grave
Jug due East and West six feet perpendicular, in the
brow of a hill where our weary brother sat down to
rest and refresh himself. Nothing was found but the
jewel of his office by which the body was designated.
King Solomon then ordered the twelve Fellow Crafts
to go and assist in raising the body, and as the Master's
word was then lost, it was agreed between himself
and Hiram King of Tyre that the first sign given on

arriving at the gi ave and the first word spoken after
the body should be raised, should be adopted as the
sign and word for the regulation of all Master's
lodges until future generations should find out the
right.* On repairing to the grave King Solomon ordered one of the Fellow Crafts to take the body by
the Entered Apprentice's grip and see if it could be
raised, but owing to the high state of putrefaction, the
body having been dead already fifteen days, the skin
slipped and it could not be so raised. King Solomon
then requested Hiram, King of Tyre to take the
body by the Fellow Craft grip and see if it could be
raised, but owing to the reasons already assigned the
flesh cleaved from the bone and it could not be so
raised. King Solomon at length took the body by the
strong grip of a Master Mason, or the 'Lion's Paw'
and raised it on the five points of Fellowship, which
have already been explained to you. They then conveyed it back to the temple from which it was buried
in due form.

"The body of our Grand Master Hiram Abiff was
buried three times: first in the rubbish of the temple,
second, on the brow of a hill west of Mt. Moriah, and
third, and last time without the gates of the city, as
near the unfinished 'sanctum sanctorum' or 'Holy of
Holies' as the Jewish law would permit; and Masonic
tradition informs us that they erected to his memory
a marble monument, consisting of a beautiful virgin
weeping over a broken column; before her a book
open, in her right hand a sprig of *acacia,* in her left
an urn and Time behind her, standing unfolding her
ringlets and counting her hair." *

* For the origin and meaning of this substitution and also the
origin and meaning of that for which the substitution was made,
see "Master's Carpet." pp. 371, 376 and 324-328.

"The beautiful virgin *weeping over the broken column*, denotes the unfinished temple and the untimely death of our Grand Master Hiram Abiff.

"The Book *open before her*, that his virtues there lay on perpetual record.

"The *sprig of acacia in her right hand* denotes the timely discovery of the body:

"The Urn *in her left*, that his ashes were there safely deposited to perpetuate the remembrance of that amiable, distinguished and exemplary character.

"And *Time behind her, standing* unfolding her ringlets and counting her hair, that time, patience and perseverance will accomplish all things."

The Master points to each of the above emblems on the chart as he proceeds with his explanation. All the foregoing it will be observed is a rehearsal of the Temple Legend, and is of course esoteric ˙or *secret work* and must be learned orally from the Grand Lecturer or other lawfully constituted teacher.

Worshipful Master (continuing): "Brother Hunt, Masonry may be said to be supported by three great pillars called Wisdom, Strength and Beauty, by which are represented our three ancient Most Excellent Grand Masters, Solomon, King of Israel, Hiram, King of Tyre, and Hiram Abiff, because there should be *wisdom* to contrive, *strength* to support, and *beauty* to adorn all great and important undertakings. These pillars you have been already informed are represented by the three principal officers of the lodge, viz.: the Worshipful Master, Senior and Junior Wardens. (See page 86.)

"The pillar of Wisdom also represents King Solomon, whose great wisdom contrived and executed that stupendous monument of architecture which immortalized his name and proved the wonder and admiration of succeeding generations.

"The pillar of Strength represents Hiram, King of Tyre, who strengthened and supported King Solomon in his great and glorious undertaking.

"The pillar of Beauty represents Hiram Abiff by whose great skill in the arts and sciences, and cunning workmanship the temple was beautified and adorned.* (The Master points to the pillars on the chart as he proceeds.)

"This magnificent structure was founded in the fourth year of the reign of King Solomon, on the second day of the month Zif, being the second month of the sacred year. It was located on Mount Moriah, near the place where Abraham was about to offer up his son Isaac, and where David met and appeased the destroying angel. Josephus informs us, that although more than seven years were occupied in building it, yet, during the whole term, it did not rain in the daytime, that the workmen might not be obstructed in their labor. From sacred history we also learn that there was not the sound of ax, hammer or any tool of iron, heard in the house while it was building. The Temple at Jerusalem was supported by 1,453 columns, 2,906 pilasters, all hewn from the finest Parian marble. There were employed in its erection 153,303 workmen, namely: 3 Grand Masters, 3,300 Masters or Overseers of of the work, 80,000 Fellow Crafts or hewers in the mountains and 70,000 Entered Apprentices or bearers of burdens. (For the three steps and classes of Emblems, see Monitor, page 48.) And all these

---

* For the meaning of this figure, see "Master's Carpet," pp. 387-388.
† App. note D. D., p. 270.
* For the origin of this emblem, see "Master's Carpet," pp. 302-308.

were classed and arranged in such a manner by the wisdom of Solomon, that neither envy, discord nor confusion was suffered to interrupt or disturb the peace and good fellowship which prevailed among the workmen.

"In front of the magnificent porch were placed the two celebrated pillars—one on the left hand and one on the right hand. They are supposed to have been placed there as a memorial to the children of Israel of the happy deliverance of their forefathers from Egyptian bondage, and in commemoration of the miraculous pillars of fire and cloud. The pillar of fire gave light to the Israelites and facilitated their march, and the cloud proved darkness to Pharoah and his host, and retarded their pursuit. King Solomon, therefore, ordered these pillars to be placed at the entrance of the temple, as the most conspicuous part, that the children of Israel might have that happy event continually before their eyes in going to and returning from divine worship.

"A lodge of Entered Apprentices was anciently composed of 7 namely: 1 Master Mason and 6 Apprentices; they usually met on the *ground floor* of King Solomon's temple.

"A lodge of Fellow Crafts was composed of 5, namely: 2 Master Masons and three Fellow Crafts; they usually met in the *middle chamber.*

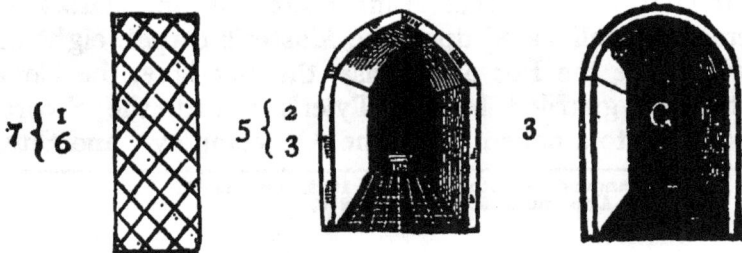

"And a lodge of Master Masons was composed of 3, namely: 3 Master Masons. They usually met in the unfinished *sanctum sanctorum* or Holy of Holies of King Solomon's temple."

THE THREE STEPS

"Usually delineated upon the Master's carpet are emblematical of the three principal stages of human

life, viz.: Youth, Manhood and Age. They also allude to the first three degrees in Freemasonry, Entered Apprentice, Fellow Craft and Master Mason. In youth, as Entered Apprentices, we ought industriously to occupy our minds in the attainment of useful knowledge; in *Manhood,* as Fellow Crafts, we should apply our knowledge to the discharge of our respective duties, to God, our neighbor, and ourselves; so that in *Age,* as Master Masons, we may enjoy the happy reflection consequent on a well spent life, and die in the hope of a glorious immortality." *

NINE CLASSES OF EMBLEMS.

Worshipful Master (continuing and pointing to the chart): "Brother Hunt, there are *nine* classes of emblems delineated upon the Master's carpet, eight of which are the Pot of incense, the Bee-hive, the Constitution guarded by the Tyler's sword, the Sword pointing to a naked heart, the All-seeing eye, and Sun,

---

* "Standard Monitor," Cook, 1903, pp. 49-50.
* See App. note E. E., page 270.

moon and stars, the Anchor and ark, the Forty-seventh problem of Euclid, the Hour-glass and the Scythe.†

THE POT OF INCENSE

"Is an emblem of a pure heart, which is always an acceptable sacrifice to the Deity; and as this glows with fervent heat, so should our hearts continually

glow with gratitude to the great and beneficent Author of our existence, for the manifold blessings and comforts we enjoy.

THE BEE-HIVE

"Is an emblem of industry, and recommends the practice of that virtue to all created beings, from the highest seraph in heaven to the lowest reptile of the dust. It teaches us that as we came into the world

rational and intelligent beings, we should ever be industrious ones; never sitting down contented while our fellow-creatures around us are in want, especially when it is in our power to relieve them without inconvenience to ourselves.

"When we take a survey of nature, we view man in his infancy more helpless an indigent than the brute creation; he lies languishing for days, months and years, totally incapable of providing sustenance for himself, or guarding against the attack of wild beasts of the field, or sheltering himself from the inclemencies of the weather. It might have pleased the great Creator of heaven and earth, to have made man independent; but as dependence is one of the strongest bonds of society, so mankind were made dependent on each other for protection and security, as they thereby enjoy better opportunities of fulfilling the duties of reciprocal love and friendship. Thus was man formed for social and active life, the noblest part of the work of God; and he that will so demean himself, as not to be endeavoring to add to the common stock of knowledge and understanding, may be deemed a *drone* in the *hive* of nature, a useless member of society, and unworthy of our protection as Masons.

THE BOOK OF CONSTITUTIONS GUARDED BY THE TYLER'S SWORD

"Reminds us that we should be ever watchful and guarded in our thoughts, words and actions, particularly when before the uninitiated; ever bearing in remembrance those truly Masonic virtues, *silence* and *circumspection.*

THE SWORD POINTING TO A NAKED HEART.

"Demonstrates that justice will sooner or later overtake us; and although our thoughts, words and actions may be hidden from the eyes of man, yet that,

ALL-SEEING EYE,*

"whom the Sun, Moon and Stars obey and under whose watchful care even Comets perform their stupendous revolutions, pervades the inmost recesses of the human heart, and will reward us according to our merits.*

THE ANCHOR AND ARK

"Are emblems of a well-grounded *hope,* and a well-spent life. They are emblematical of that divine *Ark,* which safely wafts us over this tempestuous sea

of troubles, and that *Anchor* which shall safely moor

---

* For the meaning of the all-seeing "Eye" see "Master's Carpet," p. 388. Appendix note E. E., p. 269.
* App. note F. F., page 370.

us in a peaceful harbor, where the wicked cease from troubling and the weary shall find rest.

THE FORTY-SEVENTH PROBLEM OF EUCLID

"This was an invention of our ancient friend and brother, the great Pythagoras, who, in his travels through Asia, Africa and Europe, was initiated into the several orders of priesthood, and is said to have been raised to the sublime degree of Master Mason. This wise philosopher enriched his mind abundantly in

a general knowledge of things, and more especially in Geometry, or Masonry. On this subject he drew out many problems and theorems; and among the most distinguished, he erected this, when, in the joy of his heart, he exclaimed *Eureka*, in the Grecian language signifying, *I have found it;* and upon the discovery of which he is said to have sacrificed a hecatomb. It teaches Masons to be general lovers of the arts and sciences.

THE HOUR-GLASS

"Is an emblem of human life. Behold! how swiftly the sands run, and how rapidly our lives are drawing to a close! We cannot without astonishment behold the little particles which are contained in this machine;—how they pass away almost imperceptibly! and yet, to our surprise, in the short space of an hour they are all exhausted. Thus wastes man! Today he puts forth the tender leaves of hope; to-morrow, blossoms, and bears his blushing honors thick upon him; the next day comes a frost which nips the shoot; and when he thinks his greatness is still aspiring, he falls, like autumn leaves, to enrich our mother earth.

THE SCYTHE

"Is an emblem of time, which cuts the brittle thread of life, and launches us into eternity. Behold! what havoc the scythe of time makes among the human

race! If perchance we escape the numerous evils incident to childhood and youth, and with health and vigor arrive to years of manhood; yet, withal, we must soon be cut down by the all-devouring scythe of time, and be gathered into the land where our fathers have gone before us.

"But, my brother, the last class of emblems to which I will call your attention is

THE SETTING MAUL, THE SPADE AND THE COFFIN.

"The *setting maul* by which our Grand Master Hiram Abiff was slain is emblematical of that casualty or disease by which our own existence must sooner or later terminate. The *spade* which dug his must

ere long dig our graves. The *coffin* which received his must ere long receive our remains.

"These are striking emblems of mortality and afford serious reflection for the thinking mind, but the acacia or evergreen which bloomed at the head of his grave and betrayed the place of interment is emblematical of that immortal part which survives the grave, and bears the nearest affinity to that supreme intelligence which pervades and animates all nature and which can never, no, never die.

"Thus, my brother, we close our lecture on the solemn thought of death. We are born, we breathe, we suffer, we mourn and we die. Yes, my brother, we are all born to die. We follow our friends to the brink of the grave and stand on the shore of a vast ocean, gaze with exquisite anxiety until the last struggle is over and see them sink into the fathomless abyss

We feel our own feet slide from the precarious brink on which we stand, and but a few suns more, my brother, and we too will be whelmed mid death's awful wave to ere rest in the stilly shades, where the worms shall cover us and naught but silence and darkness reign around our melancholy abode. But is this the end of man, and the expiring hope of faithful Masons? No, blessed be God, but true to our principles we pause not at our first or second step, but press forward for greater light, and as the last embers of mortal life are yet feebly glimmering in the sockets of existence, the Bible, the Great Light of Masonry, lifts the shroud, draws aside the sable curtains of the tomb and bids *hope* and joy rise to sustain and cheer the departing spirit. It points beyond the dark valley of the shadow of death and bids us turn our eyes of faith and confidence to the vast and opening scenes of our boundless eternity.

"This, my brother, concludes the sublime degree of Master Mason and nothing more remains but to deliver you the Charge which has been given to all Master Masons in every regular and well-governed lodge from time immemorial."

The Master now reads from the Monitor, or repeats orally, to the candidate, the following charge:

CHARGE TO THE CANDIDATE.

"Brother, your zeal for our institution, the progress you have made in our mysteries, and your steady conformity to our useful regulations have pointed you out as a proper object for this peculiar mark of our favor.

"Duty and honor now alike bind you to be faithful to every trust; to support the dignity of your character on all occasions, and strenuously to enforce, by precept and example, a steady obedience to the tenets of Freemasonry. Exemplary conduct on your part will convince the world that merit is the just title to our privileges, and that on you our favors have not been undeservedly bestowed.

"As a Master Mason you are authorized to correct the errors and irregularities of your less informed brethren; to fortify their minds with resolution against the snares of the insidious, and to guard them against every allurement to vicious practices. To preserve unsullied the reputation of the fraternity, ought to be your constant care; and, therefore, it becomes your province to caution the inexperienced against a breach of fidelity. To your inferiors in rank or office, you are to recommended obedience and submission; to your equals, courtesy and affability; to your superiors, kindness and condescension; and by the regularity of your own conduct, endeavor to remove every aspersion against this venerable institution. Our ancient landmarks you are carefully to preserve, and not suffer them on any pretense to be infringed, or countenance a deviation from our established customs.

"Your honor and reputation are concerned in supporting with dignity the respectable character you now bear. Let no motive, therefore, make you swerve from your duty, violate your vows, or betray your trust; but be true and faithful, and imitate the example of that celebrated artist whom you have this evening represented. Thus, you will render yourself deserving of the honor which we have conferred, and worthy of the confidence we have reposed in you. You will now step to the Secretary's desk and sign the Constitution and become a member of our lodge entitled to all its rights and benefits."

Worshipful Master (giving three raps, all the brethren stand) : "And now, my brethren, let us see to it, and so regulate our lives by. the plumb-line of Justice, ever squaring our actions by the rule of Virtue that when the Grand Warden of Heaven shall call for us, you may be found ready. Let us cultivate assiduously the noble tenets of our profession, Brotherly Love, Relief and Truth; from the square learn morality; from the level equality and from the plumb rectitude of life.

"Let us imitate in all his varied perfection, him, who when assailed by the hands of murderous Craftsman, maintained his integrity even unto his death and sealed it with his vital blood. Let us emulate his amiable and virtuous character, his unfeigned piety to God and his inflexible fidelity to his trust, and as the *Acacia's* or evergreen, which bloomed at the head of his grave betrayed the place of interment; so may *virtue,* by its ever blooming loveliness, designate us as Free and Accepted Masons. With the trowel spread liberally the cement of brotherly love; circumscribed by the compasses, let us ponder well our words and actions, and let all the energies of our minds and the affections of our Supreme Grand Master's approbation. Then, when our dissolution draws nigh, and the cold winds of death come sighing around us, and his chill dews already glisten upon our foreheads, with joy shall we obey the summons of the Grand Warden of Heaven and go from our labors on earth to eternal refreshment in the Paradise of God, where, by the benefit of the pass of a pure and blameless life and an unshaken confidence in the merits of the Lion of the tribe of Judah, shall we gain ready admission into that Celestial Lodge where the Supreme Architect of the Universe presides ; there, placed at his right hand, He will be pleased to pronounce us just and upright Masons . Then, my brethren, will you be fitly prepared for that spiritual building, that house not made with hands eternal in the Heavens, where no discordant voice shall arise, and all that the soul shall experience, shall be perfect bliss, and all it shall express shall be perfect praise, and love divine ennoble every heart, and hosannas exalted employ every tongue."

Worshipful Master: Gives one rap and seats lodge.*

---

* See also App. note G. G., page 270 for further closing.

CHAPTER VIII.

In opening the Grand Lodge at regular or special communications it is said to be opened in *ample form,* and so declared, while a *blue lodge* or lodge of Master Masons is declared open *in form.* The uniniated reader is also requested to note the distinction between the terms Master Mason and Worshipful Master. A Master Mason is simply a member of a lodge or one who has received the third degree in Masonry, while a Worshipful Master is one who is chosen by regular ballot to preside over the lodge and has been inducted into the Oriental chair of King Solomon by what is called "ancient ceremonies." As the *opening, closing* and *initiatory* ceremonies constitute each degree in Masonry, and as I have minutely exemplified the opening and iniatory ceremonies of Ancient Craft Masonry in the preceding pages, I shall now proceed to show how the lodges are closed :

CLOSING A LODGE OF MASTER MASONS.

Worshipful Master (one rap) : "Brother Senior Warden, is there anything further in the West to be brought before this lodge of Master Masons?" (one rap.)

Senior Warden: "Nothing in the West, Worshipful."

Worshipful Master (one rap) : "Anything in the South, Brother Junior Warden?"

Junior Warden: "Nothing in the South, Worshipful."

Worshipful Master (one rap): "Is there anything on your table, Brother Secretary?"

Secretary: "Nothing on the Secretary table, Worshipful."

Worshipful Master (one rap): "Has any Brother around the lodge anything to offer for the good of Masonry, or for this lodge in particular; if not we will proceed to close?"

Worshipful Master (one rap): "Brother Junior Deacon, the last as well as the first great care of Masons when convened?"

Junior Deacon (rising): "To see that the lodge is tyled, Worshipful."

Worshipful Master: "You will perform that duty and inform the Tyler that I am about to close Keystone Lodge, No. 639, on the third degree of Masonry and direct him to take due notice and tyle accordingly."

The Junior Deacon gives three raps on the door from the inside, the Tyler gives three outside.

Junior Deacon: "The lodge is tyled, Worshipful."

Worshipful Master: "How tyled?"

Junior Deacon: "By a Master Mason armed with the proper implement of his office."

Worshipful Master: "The Tyler's station?"

Junior Deacon: "Outside the inner door with a drawn sword in his hand."

Worshipful Master: "His duty?"

Junior Deacon: "To guard against the approach of cowans and eavesdroppers, and see that none pass or repass but such as are duly qualified and have permission."

Worshipful Master (one rap): "Brother Senior Warden, at the opening of this lodge you informed me you were a Master Mason. What induced you to become a Master Mason?"

Senior Warden (standing): "That I might travel in foreign countries, work and receive Master's wages, and be thereby the better enabled to support myself and family and contribute to the relief of worthy distressed Master Masons, their widows and orphans."

Worshipful Master: "What makes you a Master Mason?"

Senior Warden: "My obligation."

Worshipful Master: "Where were you made a Master Mason?"

Senior Warden: "In a regularly constituted lodge of Master Masons."

Worshipful Master: "What number constitutes a lodge of Master Masons?"

Senior Warden: "Three or more."

Worshipful Master: "When of three, of whom do they consist?"

Senior Warden: "The Worshipful Master, Senior and Junior Wardens."

Worshipful Master: "The Junior Warden's station?"

Senior Warden: "In the South, Worshipful."

Worshipful Master (two raps): "Brother Junior Warden, the Senior Warden's station?"

Junior Warden: "In the West, Worshipful."

Worshipful Master: "Brother Senior Warden the Worshipful Master's station?"

Senior Warden: "In the East, Worshipful."

Worshipful Master: "Why in the East?"*

See cut on page 36 E. P., and for the meaning of it, see "Master's Carpet." p 365.

Senior Warden: "As the sun rises in the East to open and govern the day, so rises the Worshipful Master in the East to open and govern his lodge, set the Craft to work and give them proper instruction."

Worshipful Master: "Brother Senior Warden, it is my order that Keystone Lodge, No. 639, be now closed on the *third* degree of Masonry. This you will communicate to the Junior Warden in the South, and he to the brethren, that all having due notice thereof may govern themselves accordingly."

Senior Warden: "Brother Junior Warden, it is the order of the Worshipful Master that Keystone Lodge, No. 639, be now closed on the *third* degree of Masonry. This you will communicate to the brethren that all having due notice thereof may govern themselves accordingly."

Junior Warden (three raps) : "Brethren, it is the order of the Worshipful Master, communicated to me by the way of the West, that Keystone Lodge, No. 639, be now closed on the third degree of Masonry; take due notice thereof and govern yourselves accordingly."

Worshipful Master: "Together, brethren."

The Master and all the brethren together make the due-guard and sign of a Master Mason, as explained on page 34; the Master then gives *three* raps, the Senior Warden *three,* and the Junior Warden *three,* after which the lodge is declared closed, as follows:

Worshipful Master: "Accordingly I declare Keystone Lodge, No. 639, closed on the third degree of Masonry. Brother Junior Deacon, inform the Tyler. Brother Senior Deacon, arrange the lights."

Junior Deacon: Gives three raps.

Tyler: Gives three raps.

Junior Deacon: "The Tyler is informed, Wor shipful."

Worshipful Master: Gives one rap.

CLOSING A LODGE OF FELLOW CRAFTS.

Worshipful Master (gives one rap): "Brother Senior Warden, at the opening of this lodge you informed me that you were a Fellow Craft, what makes you a Fellow Craft?"

Senior Warden: "My obligation."

Worshipful Master: "Where were you made a Fellow Craft?"

Senior Warden: "In a regularly constituted lodge of Fellow Crafts."

Worshipful Master: "What number constitutes a lodge of Fellow Crafts?"

Senior Warden: "Five or more."

Worshipful Master: "When of five only, whom do they consist?"

Senior Warden: "The Worshipful Master, Senior and Junior Wardens, Senior and Junior Deacons."

Worshipful Master: "The Junior Deacon's place?"

Senior Warden: "At the right hand of the Senior Warden in the West."

Worshipful Master (two raps calling up the last named officer): "Brother Junior Deacon, the Senior Deacon's place?"

Junior Deacon: "At the right hand of the Worshipful Master in the East."

Worshipful Master: "Brother Senior Deacon the Junior Warden's station?"

Senior Deacon: "In the South, Worshipful."

Worshipful Master: "Brother Junior Warden, the Senior Warden's station?"

Junior Warden: "In the West, Worshipful."

Worshipful Master: "Brother Senior Warden, the Worshipful Master's station?"

Senior Warden: "In the East, Worshipful."

Worshipful Master: "Why in the East?"

Senior Warden: "As the sun rises in the East to open and govern the day, so rises the Worshipful Master in the East to open and govern his lodge, set the Craft to work and give them proper instructions."

Worshipful Master: "Brother Senior Warden, it is my order that Keystone Lodge, No. 639, be now closed on the second degree of Masonry. This you will communicate to the Junior Warden in the South, and he to the brethren, that all having due notice thereof may govern themselves accordingly."

The Senior Warden conveys this order to the Junior Warden in the exact language of the Worshipful Master. The Junior Warden gives three raps, calling up the entire lodge, and communicates the same order as follows:

Junior Warden: "Brethren, it is the order of the Worshipful Master, communicated to me by the way of the West, that Keystone Lodge, No. 639, be now closed on the second degree of Masonry. Take due notice thereof and govern yourselves accordingly."

Worshipful Master: "Together, brethren."

The Worshipful Master and brethren together make the due-guard and sign of a Fellow Craft. (See pages 26-27.) The Master gives two raps and each of the Wardens gives two.

Worshipful Master: "Accordingly I declare Keystone Lodge, No. 639, closed on the second degree of Masonry. Brother Junior Deacon, inform the Tyler. Brother Senior Deacon, arrange the lights in Entered Apprentice degree."

Junior Deacon: Gives three raps.

Tyler: Gives three raps.

Junior Deacon: "The Tyler is informed. Worshipful."

Worshipful Master: Gives one rap.

CLOSING A LODGE OF ENTERED APPRENTICES.

Worshipful Master (one rap): "Brother Senior Warden, at the opening of this lodge you informed me that you were a Mason, what makes you a Mason?"

Senior Warden: "My obligation."

Worshipful Master: "Where were you made a Mason?"

Senior Warden: "In a regular constituted lodge of Masons."

Worshipful Master: "What number constitutes a lodge of Masons?"

Senior Warden: "Seven or more."

The same questions and answers follow as per page 20 from this point up to and including page 23 to question "Why in the East?"

Senior Warden: "As the sun rises in the East to open and govern the day, so rises the Worshipful Master in the East to open and govern his lodge, set the Craft to work and give them proper instructions.

Worshipful Master: "Brother Senior Warden, it is my order that Keystone Lodge, No. 639, be now *closed.* This you will comunicate to the Junior Warden in the South, and he to the brethren that all having due notice thereof may govern themselves accordingly."

Senior Warden: "Brother Junior Warden, it is the order of the Worshipful Master that Keystone

Lodge, No. 639, be now closed." "This you will communicate to the brethren, that all having due notice thereof may govern themselves accordingly."

Junior Warden (three raps) : "Brethren, it is the order of the Worshipful Master, communicated to me by the way of the West, that Keystone Lodge, No. 639, he now *closed.* Take due notice thereof and govern yourselves accordingly."

Worshipful Master: "Together brethren." (The Master and all the brethren together make the due-guard and sign of an Entered Apprentice, as on page 29.) The Master gives one rap, the Senior Warden one and the Junior Warden one, when the Master continues :

Worshipful Master: "Brother Senior Warden, how should Masons meet?"

Senior Warden (touching the miniature *level* suspended from his neck or worn on the left breast of his coat) : "On the level."

Worshipful Master: "How act, 'Brother Junior Warden?"

Junior Warden (touching the small *plumb* worn by him) : "By the plumb."

Worshipful Master (pointing to his own jewel, a small square) : "And part on the square. So my brethren may we ever meet, act and part. (Removing his hat.) And now may the blessing of heaven rest upon us and all regular Masons. May brotherly love prevail and every moral and social virtue cement us. Amen."

Response by the brethren: "So mote it be."

Worshipful Master: "Accordingly I declare Keystone Lodge, No. 639, closed in form, until its next 'stated comunication,' unless sooner specially convened in which case due and timely notice will be given by summons or otherwise. Brother Junior Deacon, inform the Tyler. Brother Senior Deacon, take charge of the lights."

Junior Deacon: "The Tyler is informed Worshipful."

Worshipful Master: Gives one rap.

The Junior Deacon informs the Tyler in the usual manner; the Senior Deacon proceeds to the altar, closes the Bible and places upon the cover the square and compass, or else they are taken charge of by the Tyler. The brethren and officers take off their aprons and jewels, which they leave on their seats to be collected by the Tyler who safely locks them up in proper receptacles prepared for the purpose, and so the legitimate labors of a lodge of Free and Accepted Masons are concluded.

It only remains for me now to add on the initiating, passing and raising of candidates, that after a man is made a Master Mason he very seldom gives himself any further trouble about learning the ritual or lecture of the third degree as he did in the two preceding degrees; in fact he is never required to learn it unless he proposes to join the chapter; and even if he were, I do not know of a dozen men in any lodge in Chicago who are capable of teaching a newly raised brother the lecture of even the first section of the Master's degree. On the night of his *raising* he takes his seat as a Master Mason, and from that time forward (unless he has ambition for office) he learns nothing further of either the origin, the history, or the ritual of Freemasonry. He is in possession of a few signs, grips and passwords and displays some Masonic emblem on his vest collar, and that is about all he knows or cares to learn of the institution. As, however, the candidate ought to be fully instructed in this as in the two preceding degrees, and especially as it forms an important part of the examination which a strange brother must undergo when he desires to visit a lodge, I shall give here the lecture of the Master Mason's degree as I have already given that of the Entered Apprentice and Fellow Craft, and thus place it within the reach of even a school boy to pass himself as a Master Mason in any part of the United States.

CHAPTER IX.

LECTURE OF THE MASTER MASON'S DE-GREE.

The following is the lecture which the candidate ought to learn after being raised to the "sublime" degree of Master Mason. This lecture, together with the first section of the Entered Apprentice degree as given in chap. III., and the first section of the Fellow Craft degree as given in chap. V., constitutes that portion of the ritual on which a visiting brother must be examined before he can gain admission to a lodge anywhere; and hence it is of the utmost importance that it should be carefully studied and thoroughly committed to memory by the Masonic student.

Q. "Will you be off or from?"

A. "From."

Q. "From what to what?"

A. "From the degree of a Fellow Craft to that of Master Mason."

Q. "Are you a Master Mason?"

A. "I am."

Q. "What induced you to become a Master Mason?"

A. "That I might travel in foreign countries, work and receive Master's wages and be thereby the better enabled to support myself and family, and contribute to the relief of worthy distressed Master Masons, their widows and orphans."

Q. "What makes you a Master Mason?"

A. "My obligation."

249

Q. "Where were you made a Master Mason?"

A. "In a regularly constituted lodge of Master Masons."

Q. "How were you prepared?"

A. "By being divested of all metals, neither naked nor clad, barefoot, hood-winked and with a cable-tow three times around my body, in which condition I was conducted to the door by a brother."

Q. "Why had you a cable-tow three times around your body?"

A. "To signify that as I advanced in Freemasonry my duties and obligations became more and more extensive."

Q. "How gained you admission?"

A. "By three distinct knocks."

Q. "To what do they allude?"

A. "To the three jewels of a Master Mason, which are the silent tongue, the listening ear, and the faithful breast."

Q. "What was said to you from within?"

A. "Who comes here?"

Q. "Your answer?"

A. "Brother James Hunt, who has been regularly initiated as an Entered Apprentice, *passed* to the degree of Fellow Craft and now seeks *further* light in Masonry by being *raised* to the sublime degree of Master Mason."

Q. "What were you then asked?"

A. "If this was of my own free-will and accord; if I was worthy and well qualified, duly and truly prepared, and had made suitable proficiency in the preceding degrees, all of which being answered in the affirmative, I was asked by what further right or benefit I expected to gain admission."

Q. "Your answer?"

A. "By the benefit of a pass."

Q. "Did you give the pass?"

A. "I did not, but my conductor gave it for me."

Q. "How were you then disposed of?"

A. "I was directed to wait with patience until the Worshipful Master was informed of my request and his answer returned."

Q. "What answer did he return?"

A. "Let him enter in the name of the Lord and be received in due form.'

Q. "How were you received?"

A. "On the points of the compass extending from my naked right to left breast, which was to teach me that as the most vital parts of man, are contained within the breast, so are the most excellent tenets of our institution contained within the points of the compass, which are Friendship, Morality and Brotherly Love."

Q. "How were you then disposed of?"

A. "I was conducted three times around the lodge to the Junior Warden in the South, where the same questions were asked and like answers returned as at the door."

Q. "How did the Junior Warden dispose of you?"

A. "He directed me to the Senior Warden in the West, and he to the Worshipful Master in the East, where the same questions were asked and like answers returned as before."

Q. "How did the Worshipful Master dispose of you?"

A. "He ordered me to be reconducted to the Senior Warden in the West, who taught me to approach the East by three upright regular steps, my feet forming the angle of a square, my body erect at the altar before the Worshipful Master."

Q. "What did the Worshipful Master then do with you?"

A. "He made me a Master Mason in due form."

Q. "What is that due form?"

A. "Kneeling on my naked knees, my hands resting on the Holy Bible, square and compass, in which due form I took upon myself the solemn obligation of a Master Mason (see page 170)."

Q. "After taking the obligation, what were you asked?"

A. "What I most desired."

Q. "Your answer?"

A. "Further light in Masonry."

Q. "Did you receive further light?"

A. "I did by order of the Worshipful Master and the assistance of the brethren."

Q. "On being brought to light what did you discover more than before?"

A. "Both points of the compass elevated above the square, which was to teach me never to lose sight of the Masonic application of that useful and valuable instrument which teaches Friendship, Morality and Brotherly Love."

Q. "What did you next discover?"

A. "The Worshipful Master approaching me from the East, under the due-guard and sign of a Master Mason, who in token of the further continuance of friendship and brotherly love presented me his right hand and with it the pass and token of the pass of a Master Mason, ordered me to arise and salute the Junior and Senior Wardens as such."

Q. "After saluting the Wardens, what did you next discover?"

A. "The Worshipful Master who ordered me to be reconducted to the Senior Warden in the West, who taught me how to wear my apron as a Master Mason."

Q. "How should a Master Mason wear his apron?"

A. "With the corner turned down in the form of a square."

Q. "After being taught how to wear your apron how were you then disposed of?"

A. "I was reconducted to the Worshipful Master in the East who presented me with the working tools of a Master Mason which are all the implements of Masonry indiscriminately, but more especially the trowel and taught me its use."

Q. "What is its use?"

A. "The trowel is an instrument made use of by operative Masons to spread the cement which unites the building into one common mass; but we, as Free and Accepted Masons, are taught to make use of it for the more noble and glorious purpose of spreading the cement of brotherly love and affection; that cement which unites us into one sacred band, or society of friends and brothers, among whom no contention should ever exist, but that noble contention, or rather emulation, of who best can work and best agree."

Q. "How were you then disposed of?"

A. "I was reconducted to the place whence I came, invested with what I had been divested and

---

*(This is Illinois work. On this point Grand Lodges differ. Some maintain that a Fellow Craft should wear his apron with the corner turned up, and others, as Illinois, that a Master Mason should wear it thus.)

await the further will and pleasure of the Worshipful Master."

Q. "From what, to what, by what, on what were you raised to the sublime degree of a Master Mason?"

A. "From a dead level to a living perpendicular by the strong grip of a Master Mason or the lion's paw, or the five points of Fellowship."

Q. "What are the five points of Fellowship?"

A. "Foot to foot, knee to knee, breast to breast, hand to back and cheek to cheek or mouth to ear."

Q. "What do they teach?"

A. "Foot to foot teaches that I should ever go on foot and out of my way to assist a needy, worthy brother; knee to knee, that in all my devotions to Deity, I should remember a brother's welfare as well as my own; breast to breast, that I should ever keep within my breast the secrets of a worthy brother Master Mason, as inviolable as my own, when communicated to and received by me as such, murder and treason excepted. Hand to back, that I should ever stretch forth my hand to save a falling brother and that I should vindicate his character behind his back as well as before his face; cheek to cheek or mouth to ear, that I should ever whisper good counsel in the ear of an erring brother and in the most friendly manner remind him of his errors and aid in his reformation and that I should give him due and timely notice that he may ward off approaching danger if within my power."

The examining brother or examining committee can ask any questions they may see fit on the second section, or dramatic part of this degree, to which the candidate or visiting brother may reply in his own words, but in strict accordance with that portion of the ritual to be found from page 175 to 223 inclusive.

Should the party under examination be *a stranger* desiring to visit the lodge and having already taken the "test oath" as on p. 39, and manifested his proficiency in the lectures as given in chapters IV., VI., and IX., he will now be carefully examined in all the grips and pass-words as follows:

The examiner, taking the visiting brother by the hand, as in ordinary hand-shaking, the following dialogue takes place, and must be literally in accordance with the prescribed formula, as this is strictly and purely the most essential part of Freemasonry.

Examiner (taking visitor by the hand): "I hail."

Visitor: "I conceal."

Ex.: "What do you conceal?"

Vis.: "All the secrets of Masons in Masonry to which this (presses the top of his thumb hard against the first knuckle near the hand) token alludes." (See figure p. 74.)

Ex.: "What is this?" (pressing with his thumb the first knuckle of visitor's hand).

Vis.: "The grip of an Entered Apprentice Mason."

Ex.: "Has it a name?"

Vis.: "It has."

Ex.: "Will you give it me?"

Vis.: "I did not so receive it neither will I so impart it."

Ex.: "How will you dispose of it?"

Vis.: "I will letter and halve it with you."

Ex.: "Letter and begin."

Vis.: "You begin."

Ex.: "Nay, you must begin.

Vis.: "A."

Ex.:   "Z."
Vis.: "Az."
Ex.:   "B."
Vis.: "O."
Ex.:   "Bo."
Vis.: "Boaz."
Ex.:   "What does it denote?"
Vis: "Strength."
Ex.:   "How is it represented?"
Vis.: "By the left-hand pillar at the entrance of the porch of King Solomon's Temple."
Ex.:   "Will you be off or from?" (Still holding the other's hand.)
Vis.: "From."
Ex.:   "From what to what?"
Vis.: "From the grip of an Entered Apprentice to the pass-grip of a Fellow Craft."
Ex.:   "Pass."

The visitor moves his thumb from the first knuckle joint to the space between the first and second knuckles; the examiner then moves his thumb to the same part of the visitor's hand. See figure, page 140.

Ex. (pressing his thumb): "What is this?"

Vis. (returning the pressure) : "The pass-grip of a Fellow Craft."

Ex.:   "Has it a name?"

Vis.: "It has."

Ex.:   "Will you give it me?"

Vis.: "I did not so receive it, neither will I so impart it."

Ex.:   "How will you dispose of it?"

Vis.: "I will syllable it with you."

Ex.:   "Syllable and begin."

Vis.: "No, you begin."

Ex.: "You must begin."
Vis.: "Bo."
Ex.: "Shib."
Vis: "Leth."
Ex.: "Shibbo."
Vis.: "Shibboleth."
Ex.: "What does it denote?"
Vis.: "Plenty."
Ex.: "How is it represented?"
Vis.: "By a sheaf of wheat suspended near a waterfall."
Ex.: "Will you be off or from?"
Vis.: "From."
Ex.: "From what to what?"
Vis.: "From the pass-grip of a Fellow Craft to the *real* grip of the same."
Ex.: "Pass."

The visitor now moves his thumb to the second knuckle, the examiner also doing the same. See figure page 142.

Ex.: "What is this (pressing hard on the knuckle)?"
Vis.: "The real grip of a Fellow Craft."
Ex.: "Has it a name?"
Vis.: "It has."
Ex.: "Will you give it me?"
Vis.: "I did not so receive it, neither will I so impart it."
Ex.: "How will you dispose of it?"
Vis.: "I will letter and syllable it with you."
Ex.: "Letter it and begin."
Vis.: "No, you begin."
Ex.: "You must begin."
Vis.: "A."

Ex.: "J."

Vis.: "C."

Ex.: "H."

Vis.: "I."

Ex.: "No."

Vis.: "Ja."

Ex.: "Chin."

Vis.: "Jachin."

Ex.: "What does it denote?"

Vis.: "Establishment."

Ex.: "How is it represented?"

Vis.: "By the right-hand pillar at the porch of King Solomon's temple."

Ex.: "Will you be off or from (still holding the hand)?"

Vis.: "From."

Ex.: "From what to what?"

Vis.: "From the real grip of a Fellow Craft to the pass-grip of a Master Mason."

Ex.: "Pass."

The visitor now moves his thumb to the space between the second and third knuckles, the examiner also moving his. (See figure, page 176.)

Ex. (Pressing his thumb as before): "What is this?"

Vis.: "The pass-grip of a Master Mason."

Ex.: "Has it a name?"

Vis.: "It has."

Ex.: "Will you give it me?"

Vis.: "I did not so receive it, neither will I so impart it."

Ex.: "How will you dispose of it?"

Vis.: "I will syllable it with you."

Ex.: "Syllable and begin."

Vis.: "No, you begin."

Ex.: "You must begin."

Vis.: "Bal."

Ex.: "Tu."

Vis.: "Cain."

Ex.: "Tubal."

Vis.: "Tubal-Cain."

Ex.: "Will you be off or from?"

Vis.: "From."

Ex.: "From what to what?"

Vis.: "From the pass-grip of a Master Mason to the real grip of the same."

Ex.: "Pass."

The visitor here looses his grip of the examiner's knuckles and again catching his right hand very firmly he presses the tops of his fingers hard against the other's wrist where it joins the hand, the thumbs of both being interlocked and pressing tightly against the hand, the fingers of each also being somewhat apart. (See figure, page 215.)

Ex.: "What is this (grasping the other's hand very strongly)?"

Vis.: "The strong grip of a Master Mason or Lion's Paw."

Ex.: "Has this a name?"

Vis.: "It has."

Ex.: "Will you give it me?"

Vis.: "I will if you place yourself in a proper position."

Ex.: "What is that proper position?"

Vis.: "The *five points* of fellowship."

Ex.: "Which are the five points of fellowship?"

Vis.: "Foot to foot, knee to knee, breast to breast, hand to back, cheek to cheek, or mouth to ear."

As the visitor mentions each point he places himself as indicated, his right foot against the other's right foot, his right knee against his knee, his right breast against his, the left hand of each on the other's back and the visitor's mouth to the examiner's ear (see figure, page 212), and in this position, still holding by the grip, *the grand omnific word* is mutually whispered as follows, and is the only position in which it can be given.

> *Vis.:* "Mah."
>
> *Ex.:* "Hah."
>
> *Vis.:* "Bone."

This ends the examination, and nothing further requires to be said in concluding this revelation of Freemasonry, but to instruct the uninitiated how to pass himself as a Mason, or to gain admission into any lodge on the face of the globe: First study carefully the initiatory ceremonies, including the *preparation* in each degree; practice the first, second and third steps as given on pages 73, 125 and 175, also the due-guard and sign of each degree as explained on pages 16, 27, 28 and 34; let two friends go over the grips and pass-words together, as explained on pages 140, 142, 177, 214 and 215; commit thoroughly to memory the questions and answers given in chapters IV., VI. and IX., also the "test oath" on page 39; study carefully and practice with the assistance of a friend the manner of giving the grand omnific word, *Mah-hah-bone,* and the strong grip or "lion's paw" on the five points of fellowship on pages 215, 216, and there is not a Mason on earth can distinguish you from a regularly made Mason, nor a lodge of Masons in the United States or anywhere else that can refuse you admission on the score of your Masonic knowledge if they did not ask for credentials should you ever make up your mind to visit one.

APPENDIX.

This is a verbatim copy of the Minutes of one of the regular meetings of Keystone Lodge No. 639 as found in the Record Book of that Lodge to-day. All the names in these minutes and throughout this first part of the Hand Book are real and are not fictious except the candidate's name.

The first edition of the Hand Book was published in 1875. All the men mentioned on page 42 were then members of Keystone Lodge. Every one of them had a copy of the book in his possession. The same is true of the members of other Chicago lodges, and if the ritual, work and lectures as given in the Hand Book are not absolutely and literally correct these men would very soon have filled the city papers with indignant denials and the country at large with unmistakable denunciations of the author. These old members of the lodge are now all scattered except Mr. Fred Becker (former treasurer). He lives at the corner of Oak street and La Salle avenue, Chicago. All the others are gone, many of them are dead and even I'm not sure that Fred Becker is still a member of old Keystone Lodge.

I am now in my 72nd year, but quite vigorous and active yet, and the Hand Book having passed through twenty-two editions and found its way into every part of the civilized world has been faithfully testifying against Masonic sham and fraud and falsehood for more than a quarter of a century. In the United States Masonry is politics and the so-called higher degrees are cultivated solely on account of the political benefit supposed to be derived from them, just as the debasing Orange system is practised in Canada West for the same reason.

At the annual meeting of the Grand Lodge of Illinois, held in the McCormick Hall, Chicago, on the first Tuesday in October, 1872, the Grand Master D. C. Cregier in his annual address made the following statement:
"As soon as possible I met with the brethren and or-

ganized a Board of Relief by appointing the following
officers and members:

"OFFICERS: H. F. Holcomb, 141, vice-president; W.
M. Egan, 211, treasurer; Harry Duval, 271, recording
secretary; E. J. Hill, 211, corresponding secretary; James
Morrison, superintendent.

"MEMBERS: T. T. Gurney, 211; D. J. Avery, 411;
John Feldkamp, 557; E. Powell, 33; D. H. Kilmore, 209;
A. M. Thompson, 311; E. RONAYNE, 639; George R.
McClellen, 141; C. J. Franks, 410; J. H. Miles, 211; John
Sutton, 310; J. E. Church, 160; I. W. Congdon, 526."

"Of this body I assumed the presidency and during
eight months I was in daily attendance at the relief rooms
with some of the above-named brethren." (Grand Lodge
Report, 1872, p. 8).

The committee to whom was referred the Grand Master's address in submitting its report recommended as
follows:

"Your committee therefore recommended the adoption
of the following resolutions:

"RESOLVED, That to Most Worshipful DeWitt C.
Cregier, president; Brethren H. F. Holcomb, vice-presi-
dent; Wiley M. Egan, treasurer; Harry Duval, recording
secretary; Ed. J. Hill; corresponding secretary; James
Morrison, superintendent and T. T. Gurney, D. J. Avery,
John Feldkamp, E. Powell, D. H. Kilmore, A. M. Thompson, E. RONAYNE, George R. McClellen, C. J. Franks,
James H. Miles, John Sutton, J. E. Church and I. W.
Congdon, members of the Board of Masonic Relief of Chicago THE GRATEFUL THANKS OF THIS GRAND
LODGE ARE EMINENTLY DUE for their self-sacri-
ficing labors in relieving the necessities of our brothers
in distress and the wisdom, prudence and zeal displayed
by them in the discharge of their sacred trust.

"RESOLVED, That in grateful recognition of the eminent
services rendered by the Masonic Board of Relief of Chicago this Most Worshipful Grand Lodge cause the report
of the commission * * * together with the second and

third of these resolutions to be handsomely engrossed, framed and PRESENTED TO EACH MEMBER of said Board of Masonic Relief."

"Report unanimously adopted."

Grand Lodge Report, 1872, p. 86.

"Representative to Grand Lodge from 639, E. RONAYNE, Worshipful Master."

Grand Lodge Report, 1873, p. 43.

Again on page 77.

"Keystone 639, E. RONAYNE mileage and per diem $6.00."

That was for three days' attendance—the entire session of Grand Lodge.

Again, "WORSHIPFUL BROTHER RONAYNE offered the following resolution which was not adopted." (Grand Lodge Report 1874, p. 77.)

"RESOLVED, That no brother living within the limits of this Grand Jurisdiction shall be permitted to visit any lodge thereof unless he shall produce to the examining committee a diploma legally attested or else be properly vouched for:"

One more explanation and official extract in this connection.

In 1872, Harmon G. Reynolds, of Springfield, Ill., was the immediate Past Grand Master of the Grand Lodge, and also publisher of a Masonic magazine called the *Trowel*. through that periodical he began at once after the great fire to solicit donations for the benefit of the burned-out Masons of Chicago and collected in all nearly $700. That money be fraudulently kept for his own use, never reporting it to the Masonic Board of Relief, and we only discovered his dishonesty by accident some time after we wound up the affairs of the Board, June 24, 1872. Seeing that he was found out, he returned a portion of the money to O. H. Miner, the Grand Secretary, and the latter at the annual session of the Grand Lodge in 1873, made a special report of the matter. Following is the report of the committee to whom that special report was referred:

"Grand Lodge Report of Illinois" for 1873, page 85:

"Your committee to whom was referred the special report of the Grand Secretary in regard to certain moneys paid him by P. G. M. Reynolds, have had the same under careful consideration, and would respectfully report that this case presents so much that is praiseworthy and noble on the part of the lodges contributing the money and *so much of an apparently opposite character in the brother who received it from them, but who withheld it from those for whom the generous doners designed it, that we find it difficult to properly express our admiration for the acts of the one, and our pain at having to refer to the conduct of the other.*"

At that same session of the Grand Lodge in 1873, I preferred charges and specifications in writing against Past Grand Master Reynolds, an incident, I dare say, unprecedented in the history of Masonry. My attack on Reynolds caused considerable excitement on the floor of the Grand Lodge, and led to many heated discussions between the friends of Reynolds and some of us Chicago Masons during the recess which was called at once on reading the charges, but at last I withdrew the paper, and John O'Neil, Worshipful Master of Blair Lodge, 393, rushing up asked me to lend him the document, which I did, but he has never returned it. This is the same John O'Neil who for some years back has been so favorably known as an expert in track elevation in Chicago. He knows that all these statements are absolutely true.

In March, 1876, Mr. Edward Cook, already mentioned in the author's preface, compiled and published a pocket Masonic manual entitled "The Standard Monitor, or Freemason's Vade Mecum," intended especially for the private use of the Masters, Wardens and other officers of Masonic lodges. That standard monitor has received the unqualified endorsement of the very highest Masonic authority in the country, as can be seen by the following testimonials, which are literal copies of the original.

"From the East of the Most Worshipful Grand Lodge of
the State of Illinois A. F. and A. M.
"OFFICE OF THE GRAND MASTER,
"CAIRO, March 27. 1876.

"Edward Cook, Esq. Grand Examiner, Chicago, Ill.:

"R. W. AND DEAR BROTHER: The MONITOR, compiled by
you, proof sheets of which have been submitted for my
examination, meets my hearty approval. It presents in a
very concise and portable form just what every Mason,
and particularly every Master of a Lodge should know;
and as it conforms to the authorized work of this jurisdiction, I have no hesitation in recommending it to the
craft of Illinois as THE STANDARD MONITOR.

"Fraternally yours,
"GEORGE E. LOUNSBURY, Grand Master."

"From Members of the 'Board of Grand Examiners,'
Grand Lodge of Illinois.

"THE STANDARD MONITOR, by R. W. Brother Edward
Cook, Grand Examiner and Grand Lecturer, will, in the
opinion of the undersigned, *entirely and fully* meet the object, which led to its compilation in furnishing to the
Fraternity, in a compact and convenient form, the means
of acquiring and imparting a correct knowledge of the
RITUAL as sanctioned by the Grand Lodge of Illinois.

"We, therefore, cordially and fraternally recommend
the work to the favor of the brethren of the Masonic Institution everywhere.

"Signed: "A. T. DARRAH, Tolono,
"IRA J. BLOOMFIELD, Bloomington,

"Grand Examiners and Grand Lecturers of the Grand
Lodge of Illinois.
"April 7, 1876."

CHICAGO, October 1, 1876.

Right Worshipful EDWARD COOK,
Grand Examiner and Grand Lecturer of Craft Masonry, State of Ill.

Dear Sir and Brother: I have examined the "STAND-
ARD MONITOR," compiled and published by you and regard

it a very desirable and important auxiliary in the establishment of uniformity of "work," as it supplies a want long felt in our jurisdiction, viz.: a text book that conforms to the Standard work and Ritual, as authorized by the Grand Lodge of Illinois. Hand Book, page 51.

I cheerfully commend the useful and convenient little volume to craft throughout the State.

Truly and fraternally yours,

DeWitt C. Creigier, P. G. M.

I heartily concur in the above.

Wm. B. Grimes,

Pittsfield, Ill., May 8, 1882.   *Grand Examiner.*

Now, the author of the Masonic Manual thus endorsed was my principal Masonic teacher, and both the Handbook of Freemasonry and Cook's "Standard Monitor," having been first published about the same time, the above endorsements will apply to one as well as the other.

The last edition of the "Standard Monitor" was issued by A. C. McClurg & Company, of Chicago, in 1903.

NOTES

Note A. "And now in humble commemoration of which august event" etc. Hand Book, p. 71. This sentence and much of what follows in the text down to the Working Tools is alleged secret work and hence in the "Standard Monitor" Cook 1903 is marked in stars or omitted altogether.

Note B. "All great and important undertakings, etc. Hand Book, p. 85. From this sentence down to the word "day,"—glory and beauty of the day,"—being alleged secret work is marked by stars in the "Standard Monitor," Cook 1903, p. 14.

Note C. "And on it we obligate newly admitted candidates" are for obvious reasons omitted from the "Standard Monitor" and their place marked by stars as usual. Hand Book, p. 87.

NOTE D. In the "Standard Monitor" we have simply: "A Lodge has THREE LIGHTS,"—the remainder of the work in the Hand Book, p. 88, being marked by stars alleging its secrecy.

NOTE E. "Lodges are situated:"—These words are all that is given of the work in the Hand Book, p. 89, all the rest about the *Situation* of a Lodge being claimed "secret work" is marked by stars.

NOTE F. At the end of the Monitorial teaching on "Brotherly Love, Relief and Truth" comes that on the *Four Points of Entrance.* Hand Book, p. 92. In the "Standard Monitor" Cook 1903, p. 21, the *"Four Points of Entrance"* are represented by four daggers thus:—

†   †   †   †

Plain enough to the intelligent Mason, but entirely hidden from the uninitiated—as they suppose.

NOTE G. In the Hand Book, pages 92 and 93, all the words immediately preceding the terms *Gutteral, Pectoral, Manual* and *Pedal* are represented by stars in the "Standard Monitor" in connection with Temperance, Fortitude, Prudence and Justice to signify that those portions of the work are secret. "Standard Monitor," Cook 1903, pp. 22 and 23.

NOTE H. We are now beginning the second section of the Fellow Craft degree being what is Masonically termed "The Middle Chamber Work." It is like all the rest of every degree work both Monitorial and Secret. It is also generally referred to as The Floor Work of the Second Degree, and is always performed by the Senior Deacon.

The placing of the candidate inside the door and between the two pillars is marked in the "Standard Monitor," Cook 1903, by stars.

NOTE I. Beginning at the words "Our Ancient brethren"—Hand Book, p. 133, down to the words "In six days God created the heaven and the earth," the entire paragraph is marked by stars as usual thus alleging the secrecy of the part.

NOTE J. PILLARS: The explanation of the Pillars given

in the Hand Book pp. 143, 144, is marked by stars in "Standard Monitor," Cook 1903, p. 32.

PILLARS.

*   *   *   *   *

for the reason already explained.

NOTE K. Passing on from The Pillars, the Senior Deacon and Candidate arrive at "The Three Steps," as described in the Hand Book, p. 134, and what follows down to "Worshipful Master, Senior Warden and Junior Warden," explanatory of the letters W. M., S. W. and J. W. on the Three Steps, is denoted in the usual manner by stars in the "Standard Monitor," Cook, 1903, p. 32, thus: "The Number Three."   *   *   *   *   *

NOTE L. The same is also true as regards this paragraph in the Hand Book p. 134, it being represented by stars thus: "The Number Five."   *   *   *   *   *   *   *

NOTE M. The Junior Warden's Station in the Fellow Craft degree is supposed to represent THE OUTER DOOR of the Middle Chamber of Solomon's Temple. Page 138 from "Who comes here?" down to the words "pass on" in the middle line from the bottom of page 140, in the Hand Book, is in stars thus   *   *   * to denote its alleged secrecy.

The Senior Warden's Station is supposed to be THE INNER DOOR of the Middle Chamber, and the dialogue carried on there is likewise marked by stars,   *   *   * in the "Standard Monitor," Cook p. 37.

NOTE N. Having *passed* the Senior Warden's Station, the Senior Deacon and Candidate are supposed to be *within* the Middle Chamber, mainly distinguished by THE LETTER G suspended over the Master's chair. All of what follows on page 143, and down to "Geometry" on page 144, is pretended to be *secret work*, and hence denoted by stars as usual.—"The Standard Monitor," Cook, p. 37.

NOTE O. These three raps are represented in the "Standard Monitor," Cook, 1903, thus o o o and the remainder of page 145 in the Hand Book is in stars * * * and thus is proved beyond any question the absolute conformity of the Hand Book to the "Standard Work," even down to 1903.

NOTE AA. There is no real Masonry beyond the Master Mason's degree. All well informed Masons know this and hence every reference to so-called higher degrees is mere nonsense. We are informed by the Past Grand Master of Minnesota, Mr. A. T. C. Pierson, that soon after the Masonic *revived* in 1717, "NEW DEGREES were created and became the rage everywhere, but more particularly in France and Germany which, became the hot-bed as it were of so-called Masonic degrees, whose name was legion. Many of these degrees were arranged in systems or rites, most of which *had their day and died out*, a few, however, became popular and have continued to be cultivated." Pierson's Traditions of Freemasonry, p. 254.

The *three degrees* are generally referred to by Masons as "The Symbolic Degrees," but in the second section of the Master Mason's degree we reach the very climax of Symbolic Masonry, and for a full explanation of what every ceremony stands for the reader is referred to "The Master's Carpet" pp. 357 to the end.

NOTE BB. It is apparent from this paragraph that the Masonic Covenant is a mutual agreement, Masonry through the Worshipful Master being *"the party of the first part"* and the candidate "the party of the second part." Masonry is selling *secrets;* the candidate is buying them. If Masonry fails to deliver the goods, and thus violates its contract, or if the solemn pledge given to the candidate in this paragraph is not true, is the candidate still bound by his part of the contract?

NOTE CC. The Secretary can use any Jewish names he pleases in this "roll call;" the names in the "Standard Monitor," Cook, 103, p. 44 are as follows:

"Abraham, Adoniram, Ammishaddai * * * * * *
Benjamin, Bazaleel, Belshazzar * * * * * *
Jethro, Josephus, Jedidiah * * * * * *
Zebulum, Zephaniah, Zedekiah

The stars being subsituted for *Jubelah,* *Jubelo,* *Jubelum* to keep the Masonic cat in the bag if possible.

NOTE DD. In the "Standard Monitor" Cook, 1903, p. 47, after naming the supports of Masonry namely, *Wisdom,* *Strength* and *Beauty* all that follows in the Hand Book on pages 226, and 227 is represented by stars * * * to give the impression of its secrecy.

NOTE EE. It will be observed that while *Nine Classes of Emblems* are mentioned, only eight are enumerated here, namely:—Pot of Incense; Bee-hive; Book of Constitutions guarded by the Tyler's Sword; Sword pointing to a Naked Heart; All Seeing Eye and Sun, Moon and Stars; Anchor and Ark; Forty-seventh Problem of Euclid; Hour-glass and Scythe. But in the "Standard Monitor," Cook 1903; p. 55, the Ninth emblem namely, "The Setting Maul, Spade and Coffin" as usual is represented by small daggers thus † † † † thereby pretending to conceal the death of The Widow's Son. Hand Book, page 228.

NOTE FF. Through an oversight, no doubt, Mr. Cook has omitted the "All-Seeing Eye" from his enumeration of the eight c asses of emblems, though he inserts it with the customary explanation on page 52 of the "Standard Monitor." Hand Book, page 231.

NOTE GG. The W. M. here gives three raps calling up the lodge, if strangers are present and wishing to "show off. "He then repeats the following as a continuation of "The Charge." Hand Book, page 238.

"And now, my brethren, let us see to it, and so regulate our lives by the plumb-line of justice, ever squaring our actions by the rule of virtue, that when the Grand Warden of heaven shall call for us, we may be found ready. Let us cultivate assiduously the noble tenets of our profession, brotherly love, relief and truth; and from the square learn morality, from the level equality, and from the plumb rectitude of life. Let us imitate in all his varied perfection, him, who when assailed by the murderous hands of rebellious craftsmen, maintained his integrity even unto death, and sealed his principles with his vital blood. Let us emulate his amiable and virtuous conduct, his unfeigned piety to his God and his inflexible fidelity to his trust. And as the evergreen, which bloomed at the head of his grave, betrayed the place of his interment, so may virtue, by its ever blooming loveliness, designate us as Free and Accepted Masons. With the trowel spread liberally the cement of brotherly love and friendship, circumscribed by the compass. Let us ponder well our words and actions, and let all the energies of our minds, and the affections of our souls, be employed in the attainment of our Supreme Grand Master's approbation. Then, when our dissolution draws nigh, and the cold winds of death come sighing around us, and his chill dew already glistens on our brow, with joy shall we obey the summons of our Wardens in heaven, and go from our labors on earth to everlasting refreshment in the Paradise of God. Then, by the benefit of a pass, a pure and blameless life, shall we gain ready admission into that Celestial lodge above, where the Supreme Grand Architect of the Universe presides, where, seated at the right hand of our Supreme Grand Master, he will be pleased to pronounce us just and upright Masons. Then shall we be fitly prepared as living stones for that spiritual building, that house not made with hands, eternal in the heavens; where no discordant voice shall be heard, but all the soul shall experience shall be perfect bliss, and all it shall express shall be perfect praise, and love divine shall ennoble every heart, and hosannas exalted employ every tongue.

The above explanation of the *Acacia* is marked by stars * * * * in the "Standard Monitor" for the reason so often mentioned already, but the very fact of stars being used to conceal one part is sufficient evidence of itself that the alleged secret part in the Hand Book is literally correct. The Monitorial part being accurate it follows beyond question that what the stars so clumsily conceal is also accurate. But referring to this general charge as a whole, the absolute anti-Christian character of Masonry could not be expressed in plainer terms, and yet Christian Ministers and Bishops are sworn to *ever* maintain and support it.

INDORSEMENT.

I have examined the within proof sheets of "Hand Book of Freemasonry," and find it is a correct exposure of Blue Lodge Masonry as is now worked in the Lodges.

THOS. LOWE,

Past Master of Grand Haven Lodge, No. 139;

Past Master of Ottawa Lodge, No. 122;

Past Master of Jenison Lodge, No. 322·

All in the county of Ottawa, State of Michigan.

www.ingramcontent.com/pod-product-compliance
Lightning Source LLC
Chambersburg PA
CBHW050213270326
41914CB00003BA/391